THE HARDEST OF
Changes

*Thankyou for
believing that I
could do this
love you
mini - me
J Ostle*

JL OSTLE

Dedication

My little family, Daniel, and Jake. Thank you for continuing to support me. You have put up with me talking non-stop about my book. I appreciate everything you helped me accomplish. I love you both so much, you are my everything.

Thank you to my friends, my beta readers. Most of you, we have recently become good friends these past few months, but you have been there, encouraging me, helping guide me, making my book the best it can be. You have listened and help me bounce my ideas. Thank you for putting up with me.

Beth Ann Miller, my new PA, thank you for my first 5-star review, thank you for sharing so much love for my book. You have helped get my books out there, being there for me. I don't know what I would have done without you.

Hannah Clarke my best friend, my new beta reader who rocks. Thank you for pinpointing the silly mistakes in the book.

Lauren Haley, I felt sorry for you when I was in the process of writing the book, asking you so many questions about storyline ideas.

Mindy McCray oh my god you have been amazing, you helped me see all the missing words that should be in my sentences. Loved all the notes appreciated it all.

Patti Washburn, you helped me fill my ego head by giving me so much praise throughout the story.

Karen Hrdlicka you have been my rock, you helped me learn so much about grammar and how to improve my writing, I will be forever grateful.

You all let me go on and on about my book. Don't know what I would have done without any of you.

The two authors that have helped me answer any questions I had. Helped guide me to some amazing people. You both are an inspiration, thank you for taking time out to talk to me, especially on your busy schedules. Chloe Walsh and Jordan Marie, thank you.

Always to my readers, without you there wouldn't be Als, Kyle and Lex. You fill me up with hope that I can do this. That I can follow my dream. Love you all.

Prologue

I can't help but smile, looking at Kyle laughing and joking with his friends. He looks so good, in his dark blue jeans and white tight T-shirt, showing his big biceps. He looks so yummy, I just want to lick him all over. As if he could sense me, he turns and stares at me, trapping me with his mesmerizing eyes. Those eyes were always my downfall, it's like he could see right through me, baring my soul to him. My whole body heats up, I just want the day to be over, so I can play out a little fantasy of mine. I walk closer to him, getting nearer and nearer, and his eyes never leave mine.

"Hey beautiful, where have you been?" Kyle asks me. Smirking at me knowing what he does to me.

"Looking for you," I say trying to keep my voice steady. God I just want him to pin me against the wall and press against me. God I have missed him, missed his touch. I have to look away for a second, trying not to show him that I was having dirty thoughts of him again.

"Here I am." Kyle leans forward and presses his lips against mine. His lips are so soft, and he's being so gentle, that I push myself against him, trying to deepen the kiss. Kyle takes the hint and grabs my waist and pulls me closer to him, I can feel his hard erection press against me. I let out a moan, not caring that his friends are nearby.

I feel Kyle start to pull away from me, I groan from the loss. When I open my eyes, I see Savannah standing next to Kyle with a huge grin on her face. She glides her hand up Kyle's arm, not breaking eye contact with me. I look at Kyle to see why he isn't stopping this. His head is turned staring at Savannah with pure lust. Smiling down at her. I take a step back, feeling hurt that Kyle would look at her like that. Knowing how badly she has treated me.

"Kyle, what are you doing?" I ask in a low voice, trying to keep calm. I see him start to stand closer to her, so their bodies are touching.

"You know my reputation, you know I can't settle with just one girl," Kyle says smiling seductively down at Savannah, then he turns to stare at me. "Als I can't help who I am, I thought you understood that?" I look at him mouth gaping open. Why is saying this?

"Yeah bag lady, you know that Kyle needs someone who has a little more experience. You honestly think a little makeover and you would be able to tame him? He has needs that I am able to fulfill." Savannah says sweetly before she wraps her arms around Kyle's neck and starts kissing him passionately. The same kind of kiss Kyle and I just shared, a few minutes before. I watch, not believing my eyes. Savannah and Kyle? I feel my heart breaking, I feel like I can't breathe.

I can't move, I'm stuck there staring at them. I see other students walking around, not paying attention to any of us. I want to walk away, but it feels like my body is glued to the spot. I see them grinding against each other. Moaning into each other's mouths. I feel my heart shattering each second, I don't want to watch this.

His hands are all over her, touching her intimate parts, then I see another set of hands grab Kyle's cheek and turn his face to their lips. Savannah watches with a smile on her face. When Kyle pulls away, I see that the hands belonged to, none other than Caitlin. My whole body starts to shake, by just watching her. She stares back at me with pure hatred that I can't help but take a few steps back, her eyes look almost black.

"You think Kyle would have chosen you? I told you before, I always get my man. He always belonged to me." Caitlin starts kissing Kyle again. Savannah starts pulling his shirt off and rubbing her hands down his toned abs, getting closer to his jeans, unbuttoning them. I get a flashback of her and Derek. Her rubbing him, as he pleasured her. I can't help the tears that fall down my cheeks.

"Kyle why would you hurt me like this? I thought you loved me?" My tears coming down heavier. They all turn to stare at me and start laughing.

"Ali, you're too innocent for me, it was a mistake trying to get more out of you. It was a challenge, now it's just getting boring. I think we should've stayed friends."

"Well you two weren't really friends, you felt sorry for her," Savannah adds in.

"She followed me around all the time, she couldn't take the hint, and what was I supposed to do?" Kyle says shrugging his shoulders. That breaks my heart even more. When I look at Caitlin, she is no longer there, with them. Where has she gone? Then I feel someone grab me from behind, holding my throat. I feel a sharp sting on my neck.

"You weren't going to win. This isn't some movie, the good girl doesn't get the guy. The guy follows with his dick, as the goody-goody moves away. You didn't take the hint, now I have to make sure you don't come back." I feel the knife graze my jaw line, down my neck. I look at Kyle, and he is feeling up Savannah, not paying attention to us. I yell his name, wanting him to help me, but he doesn't look my way. The tears start to blur my vision. Caitlin licks the tears off my face, making my whole body shudder.

"He is finally moving on with his life. He's not yours, he will never be yours. Hope this is the last image you see. The boy you love, hooking up with the one girl who treated you like the shit beneath her shoe. If you'd kept being invisible, this would never have happened. This is all your fault. This is your punishment." Then I feel two sharp pains slice through my back, causing me to scream.

I wake up in my bed, covered in sweat, breathing heavily. My mom and dad are sitting at the bottom of the bed with concerned faces. I woke them up again. I get nightmares at times, since the incident. They wake me up when they hear me scream, knowing that I'm dreaming of her. My dreams are always different, but they always end the same, Caitlin stabbing me.

"Sweetie, you sure you want to go back to school tomorrow? Maybe it's too soon." My mom says, holding my hand. I look into the same eyes that look like mine, seeing the same thing every day. Pity.

"There's no rush princess, we will understand if you need more time," Dad adds in. Pleading with me. I understand they are concerned about me, but I'm sick of the sad, pity looks I get whenever I'm in the same room as them. I want to move on, but I can't if they keep acting like I'm going to break any second. Like I'm a baby.

"I'm fine, the doctor says that it's normal to have these nightmares and that they will go away in time. I'm not putting my life on hold. I need to get back to normalcy," I say as I quickly take a sip of water from my bedside table. My mouth is so dry, it's hard getting my words out.

"If you're sure honey." Mom says before nodding to my dad.

They kiss me goodnight and leave. I know they don't want me to leave their side, but I can't be wrapped in cotton wool forever. I leave the lamp on and lay back down. First day back to school tomorrow, and I know it's going to be a hard day. I've prepped myself that the whispers and stares will happen, but I should try and ignore it. There will be a new story in no time. It takes me ages to fall back to sleep, but I'm happy that I don't have another nightmare that night.

one

I can feel the sweat slide down my neck, but I push harder. This is the only release I get, to blank out any thoughts. I keep running, till my lungs burn and I have to stop, before the point I want to collapse. I bend forward, leaning my hands against my knees, trying to get my breathing under control. When I feel my thumping heartbeat start to slow down, I sit on the grass and stare at the sun rising in the sky. The last week I've been running more and more. It turns out it's very therapeutic, especially when you have too many unwanted thoughts running around in your head.

I decide to lie down and stare at the clouds above me. Out here, I feel free. Away from my parents and my two best friends Lex and Kyle. Kyle, I guess I'm seeing, but I always find ways for us not to be alone together. I know if we are alone, I'm going to feel emotions I shouldn't be feeling, especially towards him. It's not his fault, deep down I know that, but when I see him, I see her. I've stopped running for ten minutes, and my mind is filling up with thoughts of Kyle and Caitlin.

I was released from the hospital about three weeks ago, today is the day I go back to school. I have to face the music so to speak. I can't hide forever, I know this. I was in the hospital for a week and half. I was considered lucky when the doctor spoke to me. I can still remember waking up and seeing my parents with tears in their eyes when the doctor spoke to them about the seriousness this could have caused.

"Your daughter is very lucky, considering she was stabbed twice in the back, near the spinal area. Luckily the knife didn't hit any major arteries or organs, or this could have been a lot worse. Due to the blood loss, we had to put her in an induced coma for three days, but the fluids we provided helped. The surgery to help repair the damage went well. We had to keep her sedated and intubated for several days to help her conserve energy so that she would start to heal quicker. There will be permanent scars, but she will be fine, a little weak for a while, but that is normal," the doctor says, reassuring my parents. I lay there, feeling numb, not physically, but emotionally. The doctor goes on for a few more minutes, but I sort of blank out.

"We will keep her for a few more days for observations, to make sure she gets no infections, then she can be released to go home. How does that sound?" The doctor asks me. I think I gave him a small smile with my thanks. I didn't even pay attention to him when he introduced himself. I didn't pay attention when he left the room. I kept playing Halloween night over and over. Each time, I can't help the tears I feel forming in the back of my eyes.

When I came back home, my parents moved my bed and things into the spare room, my room now. They knew I can never go back in my old room. Maybe in time, but not now. After a few days of being back home, my parents were doing my head in. They wouldn't leave my side, constantly asking if I was ok, asking if I needed anything, every five minutes. After a few hours, I was starting to get annoyed. Lex and Kyle weren't any better. They kept going on and on, I felt like screaming. I learned to pretend I was asleep when I heard anyone walk up the stairs. When my back started to feel normal, I took up running again, anything to get out of the house, away from everyone.

I stand up and start running a steady pace back home. When I get there, I see Mom in the kitchen still in her robe. It's still early. I use to hate waking up, now I hardly sleep. That's when the nightmares come. My mom was shocked when she first saw me walk through the door already awake and returning from a run, but now she is getting used to me waking up before her.

"Hi, sweetie, did you have a nice run?" Mom asks, walking towards me, as I take off my running shoes.

"It was good, going to go for a shower." I started to walk up the stairs but knew I wouldn't get very far before I get smothered again about me going back to school.

"You sure you want to go back to school, sweetie? I know you want to move on with your life, but you should make sure you're ready, and not push yourself into something you're not ready for."

"Mom, I told you this before, I'm ready to go back. If I wasn't ready, I wouldn't go. I don't know how many times we have to go through this." I say starting to get riled up, she doesn't think I can handle this.

"Just making sure sweetie. You know if it gets hard at any time just come back home. Don't feel you have to stay, if you decide it's too much," Mom says looking at me with that sympathetic face. Which has turned into something I hate looking at.

"Yes Mom, I know that. Going for my shower." I run up the stairs before she tries to say anything else. I walk into my new room, shut the door and lean against it as I slide down. I look at my new room, it's smaller, and it has less personality than my old room. I haven't put up any photos, posters, nothing. I have my bed and a desk near the window. Luckily this room has a walk in closet. It's bare, but it's how I like it. The room feels like me, empty.

I walk into the bathroom next to my room. This room doesn't have its own bathroom, one thing I do miss about my old room. I turn the shower on and wait for it to heat up. I strip out of my sweaty wet clothes. When I feel the temperature of the water is hot enough, I stand under it and let the water spray me. I stay in the shower a good fifteen minutes before getting out. When I wipe the steamy mirror, I look at my reflection. I don't look different, but I feel it. I hate that I feel like I lost part of myself and don't know how to get it back.

I know what you're thinking, why am I making such a big deal out if this? Why don't you get stabbed by someone you thought was your friend, and then think you were going to die. Tell me what emotions go through your head. She did it because of Kyle because she thought that the two of them were going to end up together. The court hearing is in few weeks, she's pleading guilty, but by reason of an insanity moment. She's taking the blame about hurting me, but she denies the photos and killing the poor dog in my bed, but all charges are on her.

Even though I'm glad I don't have to be there for the sentencing, I want to know what her punishment will be. With all the blame on Caitlin, Savannah was scott free. She got 36 hours of community service for the vandalism on my locker. I think they gave her that punishment due to the seriousness of the bullying and vandalism. They wanted her to take the whole thing seriously, even if Savannah took a small part being involved without realizing everything else that was happening.

I blow-dry my hair and keep it down. I decide to wear black denim shorts, black boob tube with my black leather jacket. I went shopping last week and got some new clothes. It was an excuse to get out of the house, it was nice. I found some cool stuff I couldn't say no to. Mom was disappointed when she saw the bags of clothes. She felt guilty for a moment but knew if she did come, it wouldn't be relaxed, it would be straining, and I didn't need that. I walk into the kitchen to get my school bag and say goodbye to my parents.

"Aren't you hungry sweetie? I made your favorite," Mom says pointing at the pancakes on the table.

"No, not hungry, but thanks anyway, I will see you after school." I walk to the front door and put on my black knee high boots.

"Princess, I know you're feeling nervous. I know you are adamant about going back to school, but if this is too much, maybe you should stay home, even for just one more week. Maybe till after the Christmas holidays." I stare at my dad, not believing I'm hearing this again.

I told Mom earlier I'm going back to school and now Dad. I'm going insane. We keep going around in circles.

"Like I told Mom, I wouldn't go if I didn't want to, now if you don't mind, I'm going to be late." I walk out the door and start to walk towards school.

I normally use to get a lift to school from Kyle, but like I said before I don't want to be alone with him, I'm not ready for that yet. I would ask Lex, my best friend for a lift, but I know she will bring up Kyle. I'm not in the mood to talk about him or answer fifty different questions. I make sure I take paths that I know are away from the main roads. Knowing my luck, I would run into either of them.

When I see the school ahead of me, I start to feel nervous. I have been ready for this day, but now facing it seems quite scary. It's that sort of feeling you get when starting a new school. You don't know how people are going to act around you. As I get closer, I can already start to feel the stares. I try and keep my eyes forward, but I can see from the corner of my eyes, people pointing and whispering. Feel like saying take a photo, it will last longer.

You can do this, don't let them bother you. You're better than their pity gossip. I keep saying to myself.

"Hey Alison," I hear someone shout, when I turn I see Derek walking towards me.

"Hi, Derek. What's up?" I look at him, and he still looks the same, his hair maybe longer, but he still looks good. I can remember why I did like him, but I can remember why I don't anymore as well.

"Just thought I would come and say hi, and see how you are doing," Derek says with a shrug. When I look at him, I don't see pity, he's looking at me like he would look at anyone else, and my body starts to relax. I haven't let my body relax in so long, I feel so strung up.

"You know, the usual, been stabbed, reading, watching television. You?" I don't know why I said that, but I feel I need to let it out.

"Oh yeah, me too, without the stabbing part. Had to rub my grandmother's feet, which is more painful than it sounds," Derek jokes, I can't help but laugh at him.

"Thanks, Derek, I haven't laughed in so long. Everyone is treating me like I'm going to break into a million pieces. Thank you for, well... acting normal around me."

"Well, I know I made shit of things, but if you ever need a friend I'm here. I wouldn't act differently around you. You don't need that. You want to forget about it, I get it."

"At least you get it, thanks, I appreciate it."

"Anytime," Derek says before glaring at something behind me, but when I feel goose bumps all over me, I know who is behind me, before needing to turn.

"Derek, any reason why you're talking to my girl?" I hear Kyle growl at Derek behind me. Five minutes being back at school, and bloody fucking drama already.

two

"**K**yle calm down, we were just talking," I say giving him a pointed look.

"Yeah Kyle, we are just talking. I wanted to see how she was doing." Derek says looking sincere as he looks at me. Kyle stands in front of me, blocking my view of Derek. Really? He is going to act this childish.

"Where was all this thoughtfulness when you were screwing around with Savannah hmm? You are a piece of shit, Ali doesn't need an asshole like you around her."

"You're right, she already has an asshole around her, you. If she didn't want to talk to me, she would have walked away. Stop thinking of you, think of her. Think of what she needs. If she wants to talk to me, she can." Derek just nailed what I was thinking. Right now Kyle is thinking about himself, feeling threatened even though he knows I wouldn't do anything, I'm still with him. I wouldn't cheat. I have two friends, only two and maybe I want someone who isn't going to treat me like I'm a baby. I can be friends with Derek if I want to, it's my choice, not anyone else's. If it ends badly and I regret it, it's my mistake.

"Kyle. Derek is right, stop thinking you are doing this for me, you're doing it for yourself. There's no harm in me talking to Derek, in a crowded hallway." I stare at Kyle and see the shocked expression on his face that I'm talking back, well I'm not going to stay quiet and let him tell me what to do. I hated when Derek did it, I'm not going to let Kyle start doing it. "Derek it was nice catching up, thank you, we will talk soon, yeah?" I give a small smile to Derek hoping he will accept my friendship.

Derek smiles back, "Anytime, I'm here when you want to talk." Derek then turns and walks down the corridor. I know I have to turn, but I'm not ready to start an argument. Not really in the mood.

When I turn, I look up into Kyle's eyes and see how dark they have gotten. He is definitely mad. Well, I don't care, I stand by everything I said. I look him in the eyes and stare back, not backing down. The longer we keep eye contact, the atmosphere changes. I can feel the electricity and heat bounce off us. My breathing starts to get heavier. Kyle stares at my chest moving faster and faster. He knows that my body is craving him. We haven't been intimate since Halloween. There had been gentle kisses, but nothing we used to do, no heat. Now I want him, so badly. I want him to take over my body.

Next thing I know, Kyle has grabbed my hand and is leading us down the hallway till we are in an abandoned classroom. He locks the door and pins me against it. His body is pressed against mine. God this feels so good, I've missed this so much. He rubs his erection against me, I can't help but moan. My panties are soaked already. It's been too long. I move my lower half so I grind myself against him, causing us both to moan. I look into Kyle's eyes and see so much hunger and want. I lick my lips waiting for his to crash against mine, when they do I feel like I'm in heaven.

My brain is switched off, the only thoughts I'm having are how much I needed this, that I need more. We are kissing like we are starving for each other. Our lips are pressing hard against each other. I grab hold of the hair on the back of his head and press him closer to me. His hands are everywhere, feeling everywhere. When his fingers slide into my shorts and past my underwear my head falls back against the door and I inhale a deep breath. His finger playing with my clit, sliding along my wet folds. My legs are shaking. Kyle leans his forehead against mine, his breathing accelerating just like mine.

He adds another finger, I feel the buildup. I open my legs a little wider and I hear Kyle groan, knowing that I have done this for him, so he could feel more of me. My legs are turning to jelly, I can feel the wetness dripping between my legs. I start to feel that ache grow more intense. Kyle rubs faster against my clit, next thing I know, my whole body shudders as I scream out my release, it feels like it won't stop, but when it does my whole body feels satisfied. It's been five weeks since he touched me. He gave me a moment to feel and forget everything that happened, till he had to ruin it.

Kyle looks at me with pained eyes. Why is he looking at me like that? Before he wanted me, now he is looking at me like he regrets doing what he did. My relaxed body is now tensing up all over again. I start to feel the anger build back up. We did nothing wrong. We are together, we are going to act like this at times, but the look on his face shows that he wished this didn't happen. I feel hurt, I felt like the old me for a moment, where everything was normal, but no, that feeling quickly left.

"Fuck, I'm so sorry, we shouldn't have done that," Kyle says, looking anywhere but at me. Great now I feel like one of his cheap whores he used to throw away.

"What, pleasing your girlfriend? Following your urges? We did nothing wrong, thank you for making me feel cheap right now," I say as I turn and try and open the door, but Kyle's hand covers mine, stopping me. His touch makes my whole body heat up again, but I squash it down, I'm too hurt to want to feel anything else.

"You know that's not it. I took advantage, I should've made sure everything was ok, not follow what my dick wants. Especially not in a classroom."

"Did you see me saying no? I wanted it just as much as you did. I'm sick of you acting like this around me. I want us to be how we used to be. I want it to be like how it was before, where you couldn't keep your eyes off me. I want you to not to be able to control your urges," I plead at him, but he looks at me with confusion.

"You know things have changed now, I want to protect you, and you haven't acted like yourself since the accident. You hardly want to be around me." Kyle whispers.

"Are you surprised? I'm trying to move on, get things back to normal, and you all act like I'm going to disappear at any second, I don't need a protector, I want my boyfriend. I want to feel wanted, sexually wanted by you. I want you to crave me. When I'm around you, you won't touch me. I'm lucky if I get a kiss from you," my voice starts to rise, I can't believe we are having this discussion before we go to class, especially after he made me orgasm.

"I do crave you, but don't want to push you into anything you're not ready for. I want to make sure you're emotionally ok. I don't want to be used as a distraction so you to forget who you are, I want you 100 percent with me, mentally," Kyle pleads. I did use that moment to forget. But that moment was for me to feel normal, that Caitlin didn't exist. I would never use Kyle like that. I love him, if being with him intimately makes all thoughts go away it's a bonus, it's not me using him, how dare he think that of me.

"You know what, if you think I would use you for any reason you surely don't know me. I was stabbed Kyle, yes I know that, it was me who had to go through all that. Now I want to move on and forget, but how can I do that if you all treat me differently. You act just like my parents. I don't need this." I pull the door open and walk out, I walk through the crowds and hope I can disappear in them. I hear Kyle yell my name, but I ignore him. I don't need to hear any more of this.

How can I have a relationship with someone who thinks I'm using them, and that doesn't want to be with me intimately? I want to be held, touched, kissed and Kyle doesn't want to give me any of those things. I may be acting like a hypocrite, I hardly see him and when I do he acts like I'm his sister. I want more than that. I spent so long waiting for him to see me as something more. He's confessed he wanted me for years and now that I had this accident he is pulling away. I'm not going through all that crap again.

I'm not going to watch him pull away from me just so he can fall into another woman's arms. I'm not going to watch another girl get close to him. I walk to homeroom and sit in my usual seat, it's still early so only a hand full of kids are here already, I can feel their eyes on me. As more people start to come in, I watch them all gawk at me before taking their seat. The one thing I knew I wasn't ready for was when Savannah walks in with her two groupies behind her. They all stop when they notice me.

The whole classroom has gone quiet to see what Savannah is going to do. I bet she will come out with some mean comeback. I sit there and wait for it. I watch her walk towards me. I can't tell what she is thinking. I can't decipher what emotion is crossing her face, when she stands in front of my desk I look up and wait. Wait for her to say something that will hurt me in one way or another.

"Hi Alison, just wanted to say, I'm glad you're doing better," Savannah says sincerely. My mouth is hanging open. That is not what I was expecting. My mind can't comprehend what she just said. I'm sure I look like a fish with my mouth gaping open.

"Oh... Ummm... Thank you," I stutter out. She gives me a smile and walks away to the back of the classroom to her seat. Her groupies are looking at me and Savannah with shock as well, at least I know it's not just me. When I look at the door again, I feel eyes on me and see Trina walk in. Another Savannah groupie. I wonder why she didn't walk in with Savannah.

"Look, who's back from the dead," Trina says, smirking at me, the whole classroom gasps in shock. I even look at her with shock. Why would she say something like that to me? "Shocked you would come back. Thought you would change schools or something, but you do like the attention don't you?" Trina sneers at me. Why is she being like this to me? Finally, I have Savannah off my back and then I gain a new bully.

"Back off Trina," Savannah says behind me, the whole classroom turns around to stare at Savannah. Savannah is defending me? I think I must still be dreaming.

"Why? Just because you have gotten soft on her. I want to show her that just because she's the most talked about girl in the whole school, she should know where she stands."

"You think you should be the one to put her in her place? I'm still the queen bee here, now fuck off. I will make sure your life is a living hell if you think you can take control. I would rather die than see you be put on top. I'm back, you got pushed back down, now stay down," Savannah says angrily at Trina, who gives a death glare back. Now I feel weird watching this interaction.

"We will see, I will take your place and be on top again, just you watch. Oh and Alison, watch your back, you never know who will be behind you." Trina takes a seat in the far corner of the room and smiles to herself.

She's doing this to act like the old Savannah to take her spot, and I get the backfire from it, great, just perfect. I turn around and mouth thank you to Savannah when she turns to look at me, she smiles and gives me a nod. I need to find out why she is being nice to me, God I feel like I'm in the twilight zone.

Lex then strolls in and looks angry when she spots me. She takes her seat and I can feel her eyes pointing daggers at me. I don't talk to her and she doesn't talk to me. Mrs. Johnson, the homeroom teacher, walks in, and everyone either starts with homework, texts or reads. I take out a book I'm reading and try to concentrate on that. I know if Lex and I do talk she will say something I don't want to hear. I'm not in the mood for another confrontation. First day, first class and what a great start. Yup, I made a great choice in coming back.

three

It was almost the end of class and Lex and I still haven't talked. We have English Lit next. I wonder if we are going to pretend we don't know each other and walk there separately. Lex has always been my best friend. I don't want to lose her, but I don't want her to treat me differently either. I should just talk to her, and tell her not to bring up past incidents, or fuss over my well-being. I finally have the plan in my head, I just need to get us talking. When the bell rings, I start to put my things away, I feel nervous, why do I feel so nervous?

"Truce," Lex says. I feel relieved that she wants to talk to me as well.

"Truce," I smile back.

"I don't like it when we don't talk, it feels too weird. I've never been so quiet in my life, I was going to go nuts in my own head." I can't help but laugh imaging how she was suffering from not talking.

"Yeah, bet it was torture."

"God yes! I thought I was going to have an outburst in class just so I can get some words out." We both laugh knowing she probably would've.

"Got some gossip for you as well," I tell Lex. Lex's eyes brighten upon the word gossip. I'm so happy that we are acting normal. This is what I wanted.

"Yeah guess who was nice to me?"

"Ummm... Some super-hot guy, who wants in your panties? You look extra smoking today. Love the biker, bad girl thing you have going on." I blush thinking I only wore it as it matched my mood, but not telling her that.

"Don't let Kyle hear you say that."

"What the biker, bad girl look?"

"No, the guy wanting in my panties," I say rolling my eyes.

"Oh my God, some guy wants in your panties?" Lex says looking shocked.

"What no, we are getting sidetracked now." I can't help but giggle at Lex

"Right ok just tell me who was nice to you."

"Savannah."

"Savannah? As in bitch-face, blow-up doll wannabe Barbie, Savannah?" Lex asks.

"Yup, the very one."

"O.M.G. I think hell just froze over," Lex says.

"You aren't going to guess what happened after she was nice to me." The look on Lex's face is priceless, she loves her gossip too much.

"There's more? Can't be as juicy as Savannah being nice, especially to you, no offense." I know what Lex is saying, I'm the last person Savannah would ever be nice too. I'm still processing it.

"Trina came in and said, and I quote 'Look who came back from the dead.'"

"She fucking didn't?" Lex looks pissed off, hearing this.

"Yup and saying that she's making sure I know where I stand in the order of things, but you're never going to believe what happens next."

"God girl, spill it already." We enter English Lit and sit in our seats and I bring my voice down so no one can hear us.

"Savannah, stood up for me and told Trina to fuck off." Lex looks at me with pure shock.

"Where the fuck was I when this was going on? I can't believe I missed all this. So Savannah finally backs off, after years of emotional abuse, to Trina treating you like shit. What has this world come to? I need to drop her down a peg or two, I'm not going through what Savannah did to you all over again. Especially now after..." Lex stops, I know who she was going to say, Caitlin.

"It's ok, you can say her name, I won't break," I say, taking my books out of my bag. I hate hearing or saying her name, but I need to get used to hearing it.

"I know you won't break, but it hurts me just remembering what she did, knowing I could have lost you." Lex final words sound shaky. I look up at her and see she's trying not to cry. I get out of my seat and hug her.

"Hey, I'm here. I'm fine, let's just never mention her, what happened or anything related. Let's talk about getting Trina off my back." I tell Lex, hoping she agrees. I don't want to talk about it, Lex obviously gets upset by it. I'm just angry at myself for letting just a memory of what happened to have so much power over my emotions.

"Deal, think you should just punch her like you did Savannah, maybe she will back off that way." I nod thinking that could work and we both laugh, I feel all the tension wash off us.

"Yeah she does throw a good punch, think she could take Trina." I hear beside me, I look up to see Savannah standing there. I'm staring in shock, will I ever get use to this?

"Yeah, so do I," Lex says looking at Savannah suspiciously.

"If she gives you any bother, let me know, I will try and sort it." I look at Savannah, she's a really good actress or she's being sincere.

"Thank you." I don't know what else to say.

"Yeah, no problem. What you've been through no one deserves to get shit after that, especially from a spoiled, jealous cow. See you around?" I nod and say my thanks again, as I watch Savannah sit in the back. I turn and look at Lex to see she is looking as shell-shocked as me. She looks at me, and I'm pretty sure she is lost for words.

The rest of the day went a bit better, I still get the odd stares, but it's either dying down or I'm getting used to it. When I start to walk towards the cafeteria, I see Kyle standing around the corner of the hallway, his back to me but know it's him. I take a step back so I can see who he is talking to. I see him talking to none other than Terri Etchers. I remember Lex telling me she was the girl who was caught making out in the boy's locker room with Chris Buyers. Why is he talking to her? I have never seen them talk to each other before.

Why do they have to stand so close? What are they talking about? All these questions running around in my head. I trust Kyle. I just don't trust her. Does that even make sense? I can see her smile at him, fluttering her eyelashes. God is she flirting with him? Then I hear him laugh. The anger is building up inside of me. Why can't he be carefree with me? Yes, I am jealous, I'm even more jealous, that once again his attention is on another girl. Probably leading her on, for all I know. I get a flashback from my nightmare of Caitlin kissing Kyle. I come back from my thoughts, and I see her rub his arm, and playing with his sleeve, looking at him, like she could eat him alive. He isn't pushing her away. Well fuck him, he acts all caveman with Derek when we were just talking, making no physical contact and he's allowed to stand so close letting another girl touch him. I walk into the cafeteria, thinking in my head *screw him*.

I walk in the line, I feel the anger build up inside of me. I hear whispers behind me, I feel like screaming at them yes I got stabbed, so fucking what? Grow the fuck up people. I feel like I'm at a zoo. Can't wait for this day to be over. Surely tomorrow will be better now that people have gotten used to seeing me. I grab a bag of chips and a Coke. Don't feel that hungry. When I pay, I look around the tables. Not sitting at Kyle's table, fuck him. I may be childish, but I don't care. I don't see Lex anywhere. I see Derek though, so I make my way towards him. Kyle has no right in judging me after I saw him being all cozy with what's her face?

"Hi Derek, is it ok if I join you?" All his friends look up at me and stare. Never felt so uncomfortable in my life.

"Yeah, of course," Derek says as he helps pull a seat out next to him. I sit down and see that all his friends are still staring at me.

"What up Ali? Looking especially hot today." I look opposite me to see Tom, one of Derek's friends who I met at Mitch's party. He gives me a wink, my body relaxes, as everyone starts accusing Tom of wanting to get in every girls panties as I'm the fifth girl he told looked especially hot today. I can't help but laugh along with their conversation passing between them.

"What? I am not allowed to tell hot girls they look attractive?"

"Not when you only say it to try and get in their panties," a guy with a buzz cut says next to him. Heard Tom call him Nick before.

"Some girls don't wear panties," Tom says, we all groan at him. This feels so normal and fun, I'm glad I decided to sit here.

"Ali, what you doing sitting here? Thought you would sit at my table like normal," I hear Kyle say behind me. Now he wants things to be normal. I turn around and glare up at him.

"No thanks, I'm sitting here today, if you couldn't tell by our laughter, we were enjoying ourselves. If you don't mind." I say and turn back around. I can still feel Kyle's staring at the back of my head.

"Ali, why are you doing this?" Is he trying to make a scene? I don't want to be at that table, especially after he was being all close to another girl. I'm pissed enough. Doesn't he know when a girl is pissed off they need space? He's never been used to me acting like this with him, but I'm not going to be his doormat. One rule for him and a different rule for me.

"I'm not doing anything. I want to spend my lunch with people who are treating me like a human being. Not someone they feel sorry for. I will talk to you later." I don't even look at him, I say it with my back still turned. I know if I turn around I will succumb to his sweet pleading eyes or I will be so angry with him, I will blow it out of proportion.

"Fine," Kyle says before I hear him walk off.

"You ok?" Derek asks. I nod and apologize to everyone at the table for my drama, but they all wave me off and talk amongst themselves again. Thank God.

"You know you can join us for lunch whenever you want, never feel you have to ask." I look at Derek and smile at him. He is being so nice. I'm glad we are friends. I feel normal around him, right now this is what I need. Being around people who don't treat me any different, asking me if I'm ok every two minutes. Being here with them isn't connected with Caitlin.

I start eating my lunch and catching up with Derek. We fall into comfortable conversation. We laugh at Tom, at some of his outbursts, he reminds me of a male version of Lex with the no mouth filter. Wonder where Lex is? I look around the cafeteria and I see Savannah laughing with her friends. I look at Derek then back at her and remember what I walked into about six weeks ago. Shocking how quickly time has flown. How different we are now, in just a short time frame. That's life though isn't it? Growing, changing. I realized though after my little getaway at the spa for my little makeover, sometimes change ain't a good thing. I know that more than anyone.

four

After school was over I was staying put in the hallway deciding on what I wanted to do. I know I don't want to get a ride from Kyle. I just can't bring myself to ask him. I decide to just walk home. Walked this morning, can walk back. I start to head towards the doors I see James, Lex's boyfriend. Maybe if he's driving Lex home, he wouldn't mind giving me a lift too. I want to have a run when I get in and know if I walk all the way home, I would be tired after running a mile or two. I yell James's name and pick up my pace when he turns around, surprise on his face knowing it was me shouting out to him.

"Hi Alison, everything ok?" James asks.

"Yeah, just wondering if you're giving Lex a lift home today?" I say sheepishly, I feel like maybe this wasn't such a good idea, hardly talk to him and I'm going to ask for a favor.

"Yeah, meeting her at my car now. You want a lift?" I feel so happy that he has offered, thinking about walking has put me off actually doing it.

"You sure you won't mind?"

"I wouldn't offer otherwise, plus Lex would kick my ass too,"

James chuckles and I laugh with him. "Come on, she's probably wondering what's taking me so long."

We walk side by side, heading towards his car in the parking lot, I have never been so grateful he parks opposite side of the parking lot from Kyle's car. Don't think Kyle would be impressed knowing I'm getting a lift from someone else, knowing he is the one who takes me home. When we get closer to James's car, I see Lex leaning against it, looking like she is posing for a magazine. She is stunning, looking at James' face, he thinks so too.

"Als, what you doing here? Everything ok?" I'm starting to dislike that question now.

"Yeah, James was kind enough to give me a lift home. You don't mind do you? I can walk." I will walk if I am in the way. Didn't think maybe them two wanted to be alone, God I can be so selfish.

"Don't be silly. Does Kyle know?" Lex asks as we all climb into the car.

"Ummm... No, he doesn't. Not in the mood to talk to him. By the way, what happened to you at lunch? You never showed up." Lex blushes and looks down. She never blushes. James chuckles quietly, we drive off heading to my house.

"Well I got a little distracted," Lex says, not looking at me. It takes few minutes for it to click. She was hooking up with James somewhere. Well, that explains it. They can't keep their hands off each other. With that, I feel a lump build in my throat. That is what Kyle and I were like. Now he doesn't even want to touch me without feeling guilty. "You didn't mind did you? Thought you would be sitting with Kyle at his table. You didn't sit on your own did you?" Lex asks all concerned. Great now I have to tell her about Derek. Please, please, please don't overreact, I plead to myself.

"Well I didn't sit with him as I caught him talking to Terri Etchers, and they were being very friendly," I say obviously showing my distaste.

"What the locker room hook up? What was he doing with her?" Lex says showing her dislike with this situation too. At least I know she has reacted like me about it.

"Yup and she was touching his arm and batting her eyelashes at him, He didn't even move away, he was laughing with her and everything."

"What the fuck? Has he not learned from the..." Lex pauses but continues knowing we both need to move forward from this uncomfortable subject about Caitlin. "Caitlin thing. He's talking to other girls, who obviously showing interest. He's with you, he needs to set people straight, not encourage it." Lex says sounding pissed off. This is why I love her, she gets me. I'm so glad I wasn't being childish about this, Lex would have told me if I was being stupid about it.

"Maybe, he was just being nice and didn't think anything more of the situation?" James adds in. Lex looks at him with shock on her face. She obviously doesn't like his opinion.

"Terri is a girl who hooks up with random men in the guy's locker room for thrills. She was touching him, which shows she wants him. After everything with Caitlin, he shouldn't act like that around girls. This situation is totally different, due to what happened." Lex explains.

"I know babe, but the whole thing with Caitlin was bad, I get that. I was there with you, holding you when Ali was in the hospital. I was there through every tear. But it's like lightening striking at the same place twice, not every girl is going to do what Caitlin did, just because Kyle talks to her. I'm not being mean Ali I swear, I just don't want these thoughts going through your head every time you see him with a girl. It will drive you crazy with worry." James finishes and me and Lex just gawk at him. I appreciate he didn't pussyfoot around it. I needed to hear it straight. Is he right though? Am I looking too much into it?

Yes I'm worried that another girl will end up like Caitlin, but James is right, it's not like it could happen again. There must have been something wrong with Caitlin to start with. The thing I hate though is how close Kyle and Terri were being. That's a normal girlfriend reaction.

"James," Lex hits James's arm, in shock he would come out with that.

"No Lex, he's right. I want to have normal conversations, not act like we are walking on eggshells. I appreciate your honesty, James. I know not every girl is going to hurt me like Caitlin did, but Kyle doesn't want to be intimate with me. He doesn't even want to touch me. With Terri, he was being all close and relaxed. He hasn't been like that with me since the Halloween party." I slump against the back seat.

"I'm sure that's not true, it's obvious how much he loves you," Lex says.

"This morning he went all caveman because I was talking to Derek..."

"Wait you were talking to Derek?" Lex screeches at me. Oh, bananas.

"We'll get back to that. Anyway he took me into a classroom and we fooled around, but after he was apologizing, looking at me with such guilt for touching me, I felt used. I felt like one of his dirty used women."

"Oh Hun, I'm sure it wasn't that bad."

"It was. He thinks I'm going to use him sexually to forget about Caitlin and stuff. I couldn't believe he would think I would use him in any way. Doesn't he realize I need to be held and loved? He is pushing me away. I can't go back watching him be friendly towards other girls and me watch it happen. I won't do it." I may be sounding whiney, but I don't care. I need all this out.

"You need to talk to him, tell him how you feel. He needs to know what's going around in your head. Tell him what you want. If you both can't move on from it, maybe..., maybe you should take a break from each other." I know Lex is right. It took me so long to have Kyle and now I might have to give him up if we can't get back on track. We sit quietly for a while, all of us digesting what we have been talking about.

"Now tell me about Derek," Lex breaks the silence. I can't help but giggle, thinking how long she had to wait before she cracked.

"This morning, he came over to see how I was. We weren't touching or flirting like Kyle was. Kyle acted like Derek was feeling me up in the middle of the hallway or something. Then at lunch..."

"You saw him at lunch too?" Lex interrupts.

"Stop interrupting, I'm telling you now," James chuckles. "After seeing Kyle being all lovey dovey with Terri, I walked into the cafeteria. I didn't want to sit with Kyle after that, so I was looking for you, when I couldn't find you, I saw Derek. So I asked to sit with him and his friends. They all treated me like I wasn't the bearded lady. I felt normal. Kyle comes over and asks why I wasn't sitting with him, but I was still angry seeing him act like his old self with another girl. So told him I wasn't moving and I would speak to him later." God I haven't talked this much in weeks. I take a deep breath in and relax. Lex is looking at me, picking her words carefully. I know she isn't going to like the whole Derek thing.

"Right no pussyfooting, be careful when it comes to Derek. I don't want him thinking he has a shot with you, especially after what he did with Savannah. Kyle is being an ass, but talk to him. You need to know what is going on with him. Can't believe how much drama you went through today, it feels like you are in a soap opera or something." Yeah, I couldn't agree more. Too much drama, for my liking.

We talk about James and Lex's day, something less dramatic. All too soon I'm home. I know I'm going to get a billion questions about today when I walk through that door. I lean forward and hug Lex, she hugs me tightly before letting go. I look into her eyes and still see a little sadness in them, all I think about is what James said about him being there when she was crying for me.

"I love you, Lex."

"Love you too," Lex says and her lip trembles a little. We hug one last time before we let go. I pat James on the shoulder and thank him for the lift, he replies with anytime. Good to know. I walk out of the door and wave as they drove off. I look at Kyle's house and notice his car isn't there yet, part of me is grateful as I was scared he would be waiting for me. Now part of me is wondering what he is doing? Who is he with? God that boy drives me crazy.

I walk inside and it smells amazing. Mom is in the kitchen cooking our dinner. Part of me wants to run to my room, but I know she would come up to see how my day was anyway, so better get it over with now. I walk into the kitchen and see her cutting vegetables and things up. When she sees me, she stops what she is doing and runs to me hugging me to the point I can't breathe. When she releases me, she holds me at arm's length, making sure I'm not harmed.

"God sweetie, so glad your home. Is everything ok? Did anything bad happen? Was anyone mean to you? Was Savannah giving you any hassle?" Mom asks without taking a breath.

"Mom I'm fine, everything is fine." Not in the mood to talk about the stares and whispers. Definitely not going to mention about Trina, she will worry over nothing. I will deal with Trina eventually. Not going to let another person bully me.

"Maybe it's too soon for you going back to school. I have been worried sick all day. Why don't you have the rest of the week off? I will call Mr. Phillips now." Mom says grabbing the house phone. I roll my eyes on how ridiculous this is.

"Mom I told you I'm fine, I'm going back. This is my decision." Mom looks at me like I'm going to have a break down at any second. I need to get away. I walk away from Mom's reach and tell her I'm going for a run. She tries to ask more questions, but I run up the stairs not giving her a chance. I need a long run. I need to get away from this house.

five

I put on a pair of shorts, a T-shirt, and a hoodie and leave the house before anyone can talk to me. I need to clear my head. As soon as my feet hit the pavement, I go for a slow paced run. I feel the wind blow in my face, I feel like I can breathe again. Stepping into that house, knowing Caitlin somehow found access, slaughtered a dog in my old bed still haunts me. Just knowing how easy it was for her to enter my home, the home I grew up in. My mind starts to clear, emptying all thoughts.

I don't know how long I've been running, but I keep going, the sun has started to set but yet I don't stop. This is the only time I feel at peace with myself. I start to feel my legs get to the point where I'm about to buckle to the ground so I sit down on the nearest bench and catch my breath. I look around me and realize I am on the opposite side of town, near the park. Parents are taking their children back home as it starts to get dark. I look at their happy faces and feel jealous of them. They aren't traumatized, their thoughts are all happy and innocent. My thoughts are screwed up. I want to get back to where my only concern is hiding my body so I wouldn't get taunted, now I realize how stupid and childish I was.

I remember not looking in the mirror afraid of what I may see. I start to feel the anger build up in me. I want to go back, I want to go back where my only concerns were worrying about my feelings for Kyle and dealing with Savannah. I think about my little obsession with him, and think I probably wasn't better than Caitlin. She was his friend and hoped to be with him. Did he try it on with her at any point? Lead her on to think they had a chance down the line somewhere? All these questions nagging at me.

I get up and decide to walk back home. My legs are a little sore, there's no way I could run back. On the walk back, I wonder what I would have done if Kyle ended up in a relationship with someone else. I was used to his hook ups as I knew they didn't mean anything, but what if he decided to be with someone else romantically? Would I of ended up like Caitlin? I knew my answer was no. I couldn't have done what she did. But I do know my heart would have been broken seeing him fall in love with someone else.

I have Kyle and yet I don't feel like I really do. He isn't acting like himself around me. I want my best friend back. I want him to be playful with me. I missed his lustful stares, how he use to touch me, craving me. I still see the image of him and Terri in the hallway repeating over and over in my head. I have never seen him talk to her before. He definitely has never mentioned her, so she was either a past hook up or... I don't want to think of the latter. When I see my house come into view, I feel dejected. I feel like I'm walking back into a prison. I know my parents are concerned about me especially knowing I'm not acting like my old self, but neither are they.

I don't like knowing I have to go into that house. I know I was living with Kyle temporarily after the dog thing, but after the hospital, my parents wanted to look after me. Kyle still had school, he couldn't put his life on hold till I got better. He didn't even fight it. You read in books or watch in films where the boyfriend argues that he can manage and he doesn't want to be away from his girl, but not Kyle, he agreed. I know it was for the best and I couldn't ask of that from him, but I wish he wanted to stay by my side.

The more I think about it, I know he is starting to push me away. Maybe not deliberately but he is. I have sensed it for a while and I think that's why I can't stand to be around him. When I am, he builds this wall up that I can't get through. I feel tired from all this Kyle chasing. I wanted him for years, but I'm not going to try and change his mind anymore. I shouldn't have to. He should try and be with me, but he doesn't. I feel like he's already given up on us. With that, I make the decision. I'm going to end things with Kyle. I need to focus on me, and me moving on. I can't keep thinking over and over about Kyle and what he's thinking, what he wants. I love him, it's going to break my heart, but I know it's for the best.

When I'm a few feet away, I look over at Kyle's house and still no car. No lights are on. That is the final nail in the coffin. He has stopped caring. He obviously still cares for me, I'm not denying that, years of friendship you can't stop caring, but he has stopped wanting me. I see that. If it were the other way round, I would be calling and banging on the door making sure he is ok, demanding we talk. Kyle is making this easier for me. I'm going to tell him at school, we are over. He can't make a scene there. I know he is going to argue against this, but deep down I know he will be relieved. He can move on with his life, not pitying me and what I'm going through. I still have Lex and I gained Derek, and his friends have accepted me into their group. I'm finally going to make a fresh start.

The next day, I get Lex to pick me up. I text her the night before telling her I made the decision to end things. I tell her he made no contact with me yesterday. He wasn't home till quite late. She asked me if I knew where he went but told her I had no clue. Even though we were texting, I could sense the unease from her. I feel it myself. The questions running around in my head. The thing that hurts the most is thinking if he is being intimate with someone else, even though he is meant to be with me.

Lex arrives twenty minutes earlier than normal, as I don't want to run into Kyle. I am waiting till school before I talk to him. Yes, I am a coward and probably doing it in a childish way. It's the only way I can be strong enough to do it, is doing it at school. I hear Lex downstairs talking to my parents. I hurry and finish getting ready so I can take her away from their scrutiny. I walk to the landing and hear my mom asking Lex how I've been.

"I'm just worried about her. She doesn't talk to me anymore. She runs for hours, hardly eats, I feel like she's trying to put herself into an early grave," My mom says, sounding like she's trying not to cry.

"I know mama two, this is her dealing with this. You need to let her move on from all of this in her own time. If we keep holding her, she's going to push harder away. Give her time," Lex says. Least she knows I need my space.

"It's just hard, but I get what you are saying. We need to stop smothering her, just hope she can come to us when she needs us, that's all."

"She knows that, just let her be, let her come to you." I start to walk down the stairs, I'm starting to feel claustrophobic again.

"You're such a good friend, glad my baby has you," Mom says hugging Lex. I do a little throat cough so they know I'm here.

"Ready Lex?" I ask.

"Ready, see you soon." Lex hugs my dad and mom and she walks towards me, we head to the door. I yell goodbye over my shoulder and start to head to Lex's car.

"Have you heard anything from Kyle?" We open the doors to get in her car. I sigh as I get in.

"No." I look towards Kyle's house and see his car, in his usual spot. At least I know he came home last night.

"Can't believe he is being like this. I know you two are having your problems, but after everything you have been through, he's acting like it just only happened to him," Lex says angrily as she drives away towards school.

"I am part to blame as well, I have been avoiding him at times... well ok, quite a lot, but it's just because he acts differently around me.

When I look at him, I hate what I see, the pity on his face, the same looks my parents give me every single time I see them. How am I meant to move on if no one will let me, it's been five weeks, they act like it just happened a few days ago or something," I rant. I need to get all this out.

"They thought you were going to die, I thought I lost you. Seeing you in Kyle's arms, all that blood..." Lex pauses, wiping a few tears away. "When you didn't wake back up, we thought we lost you. They are going to take time before they will act normal again, well as close as normal as parents can be. With Kyle, I know it hit him hard, but the way he is acting, I have no excuses for him." I give Lex a side hug, she pats my hand as she drives. I sit back in my seat and take a deep breath.

"It's not just my parents, it's that house. I have to move to a different room. That house feels different now, I can't explain it. My parents want to lock me up and keep me away from the world. I just can't breathe there with them hovering over me."

"I can't imagine what you are going through, but remember I am here for you. Never bottle it in. And please don't push me away. It hurt that you hardly spoke to me. I hated that Kyle picked me up yesterday and you weren't there. You didn't text, or ring either of us to say you weren't coming with." God I have been a sucky friend. I never thought about her feelings, just my own.

"I know, I'm really sorry. You had the same look as them, couldn't handle seeing it. But you're acting like you around me again, and I need that. I need normalcy."

"I get it, no acting weird. Now back to Kyle, you really going to end things with him?" Lex asks.

"Yeah, we aren't the same people we were. We are pushing each other away. I don't know what his reasons are, but I am not sitting back and watching him go back to his old ways. I am not going through that, with all this..." I wave my hand around indicating everything, "in my head. If he wants to start being all cozy with other girls, I'm not going to stand by and watch."

"I get it, you don't deserve that. He's being a complete knob. What about you and Derek though?" Where did that come from? I told her we are just going to be friends.

"We are friends. I told you, he acts like his normal self around me. I am not going to date him again, I'm not that stupid. Plus I'm not ready for that. I remember what he did with Savannah and the little things that bothered me, so nothing to worry about."

"Ok, good." We talk about her and James, and Christmas that is coming up. When we get closer to school, I start to feel nervous. Today is the day I end things with my best friend. I feel an ache in my chest, I start to rub it. I have to do this. It's best for the both of us. Why do I feel like I'm going to make a huge mistake?

six

Lex and I stay in the car, talking through my plan. I am going to wait for him to arrive and join his group of friends. Going to pull him aside, and tell him we can't be together romantically anymore. I know he won't make a scene in front of everyone. I know, I'm a coward, I said this before, but I can't handle confrontations. When I see Kyle park and get out of his car, my breath catches in my throat. He looks so hot, I feel tingles all over my body just looking at him. God this is going to be harder than I thought.

"You sure, you want to do this? You could give it more time." Lex says. I shake my head. I need to do this. It's for the best. I say it over and over as I get out of the car and walk towards Kyle.

"Kyle can I have a word?" I'm pretty sure my voice sounds shaky. I'm trying to act calm, but my mouth is going dry. I'm getting a somersault of butterflies in my stomach.

"Now you want to talk to me? You didn't want to talk yesterday. You wanted to stay with that asshole Derek," Kyle glares at me. So much for me thinking he wouldn't cause a scene. I start to get angry.

He's acting like somehow I'm in the wrong when he was flirting with another girl. But he doesn't know that I saw it with my own eyes. The dick.

"Don't you dare, raise your voice at me, you asshole. Least Derek is showing that he cares, as you flirt with other girls, and doing god knows what. You have made this easier you prick," I seethe. I feel all that anger build in me. I see Lex stand by my side, holding my arm for support, at least I know she has my back.

"Kyle how fucking dare you treat Als like this. She is going through some shit, and you're acting like a pure idiot, and that's putting it mildly," Lex says stabbing her finger at Kyle's chest.

"Stick your nose out of this Lex, this doesn't concern you. She is going through shit? What about the rest of us? Huh?"

"You selfish asshole, we aren't the ones that got stabbed by a girl you lead on. By the girl who was obsessed with you. This is you all over. I don't blame Als if she blames you. You're a piece of shit. You hook up and screw any girl that opens her legs for you, you didn't expect any consequences? Als almost died, you treat her like shit after it, cozying up with fucking attention seeker Terri Etchers. You did it in front of Als." Lex breathes in, ready for another shout out.

"You have a fucking nerve to yell at her for just being friendly towards another guy," Lex yells in Kyle's face. A crowd surrounds us, watching. So much for not causing a scene. I look at Kyle and the look on his face, looks like someone sucker punched him in the chest.

"I... How dare you, blame me. I know she almost died. I held her when she was begging not to die. I was there." Kyle yells back

"Yeah! So was I, you don't see me, shitting all over her. So what? You got bored and wanting to start sticking your dick in everything again? Don't bring Als down with you." I hold onto Lex's shoulder and pull her back so I can look Kyle in the eyes when I say this to him. Lex is right deep down, it's not just how he looks at me that I get angry at. I blame him for Caitlin, I blame him how he treats girls. I held him on a pedestal. I didn't see that he was just like any other player at this school. I saw it all along. Him bringing girls back to the car. Him hooking up with girls at parties. He never denied it. I let it slide, I was blinded by my love for him, and I just didn't care.

"Lex it's ok, I got this," I say as I step up to Kyle, I see him tense up and hold his breath. I look into his eyes. My whole body involuntary shivers by how intense they are. I am always going to love him, my body is never going to stop craving for him. I see the look in his eyes change, my breath catches, and I can tell he heard it. The electricity between us changes, I can tell he feels it too. I need to do this now before I cave in. I can't keep going on like this. I can tell he notices something is wrong when I look him in the eyes once again. Holding back all my emotions, is what I need to do now, I can't let the hurt of doing this show. I start to bring up all the coldness and hate I feel for him. It's unfair, but I need all the anger I have so he knows I mean what I'm about to say.

"Kyle, Lex is right. I have been distant because I am going through all this chaos in my head every single day. Part of me blames you for what I went through. You treat girls at this school like they are nothing. You make them think they have a shot with you and then you throw them away like yesterday's trash. I blame you for leading Caitlin on. You lead me on, by all the secret touches, all the intimate words you gave me behind closed doors. Part of me can't forgive you for treating her like you treated me. I saw you yesterday with Terri Etchers when I was heading to the cafeteria..." Kyle looks pained for what I'm saying, but I keep going, I have to. "...I saw how different you were with her, you haven't acted like that with me in a long time. Then you have the cheek to go all caveman on me because I was at a table surrounded by others talking and laughing. You were alone with another girl, yet you thought what I was doing was wrong. You didn't contact me at all yesterday. You didn't show any indication that you care. Maybe you do, but I haven't seen it. Yesterday we had a moment, yes it made me forget all my problems, but I loved that I was with you. I was close with you, but you hurt me. You hurt me by saying I would be able to use you. You know me better than that, yet you still said it. Is it really a bad thing that I know you are the only one that can take away all the pain that I'm feeling?" I take a deep breath knowing that this is me finally ending it.

"I can't go on like this anymore. I can't be with you, not romantically. Maybe someday we can go back to being friends but right now, I need my space away from you," I take a deep breath and take a few steps back. I look back into his eyes I see he has closed himself off to me. It takes a lot for me not to cry.

I link my arms through Lex's and start to walk away, but as we start to walk off Kyle grabs my arm. I turn, I wait for him to say anything. He doesn't. I nod, then pull my arm out of his grasp, he lets me go. Lex guides me to her locker, and part of me feels numb. Lex hasn't spoken yet, giving me time to digest everything that has happened. The look in Kyle's eyes. He has put a wall up again, blocking me away. I can't believe where we are. Years of friendship, closeness, gone. I can feel the tears build up behind my eyes, Lex looks at me and knows I'm about to break down. She guides me to the girl's restroom and when we get into a stall, my tears break free.

Lex holds me, giving me encouraging words that are for the best, that I did the right thing. All I see is all the flashbacks of me and Kyle running through my head like a movie. He and I chasing each other as kids. Us wrestling in the mud in the rain. Him defending me against Savannah. Our Friday night traditions. God no more Friday nights. I see him hold my hand in his car, smiling at me. Our first kiss, him touching me. The tears fall down harder.

When my tears have stopped, Lex guides me to the sink and starts wetting some paper towels and dabbing them under my eyes, trying to get rid of the puffiness. I give her a small smile in thanks, which she returns. We have missed homeroom, but I don't care. I thought what Caitlin did to me, was the most painful thing, but this is. I didn't just end things with my boyfriend, I lost my best friend. Lex lost a friend too. I know she chose my side. I never wanted her to lose a friend. I never wanted her to choose, but she did. I feel selfish hating that I'm happy she chose me.

I felt my body go on autopilot through my classes. I just felt I was in some sort of daze. When it came to lunch time, Lex was waiting by the doors, with James. She hugged me and linked her arm through mine as we waited in line to get our food. I'm not hungry, but I grab a sandwich and a Coke. When we head towards the tables, my first reaction is to look at Kyle's table. He isn't there, part of me is relieved as it would be harder knowing he is in the same room as me, but part of me is wondering what he's doing and who with. I have no right anymore, but it's going to take time to get used to.

I see Derek's table and there's a couple seats empty, Lex must sense where I am looking 'cause she sets her lips in a thin line but guides us to his table. I sit next to Derek, and Lex sits by my side. James pulls a chair from another table and sits by Lex, they start up a conversation, and I hardly pay attention too. I feel drained, I feel numb. I keep thinking in my head if I made a huge mistake, but deep down another voice is telling me, we would have hurt each other if we continued, it's better this way. Just hope that voice is right.

I look around the cafeteria and seeing people laugh, talk, and going on with their lives as I feel that mine is breaking, crumbling around me. I don't like being home, I lost my best friend, and I feel that I'm having an out of body experience. I can feel the tears prickle behind my eyes again, I don't want to cry. I haven't got the energy to cry again. I feel something touch my hand. I look down and see Derek entwine his fingers with mine. He gives me a small smile. He knows I'm about to break, and he gives me this small gesture of comfort. I shouldn't let him hold my hand, but I haven't got the strength to say no. This little gesture helps me calm down. Grounds me. Throughout lunch, I let my hand stay in his. I know this is wrong, but part of me doesn't care anymore. I need this comfort, I need this security of feeling wanted, cared for.

seven

Before I know it, it's Friday morning. This week has been the hardest for me. Kyle and I act like we are complete strangers, we don't acknowledge the other person. I don't know what I was expecting, but I didn't expect this. I see Kyle going back to his old ways, flirting with girls, being all touchy, touchy. It just shows I must have meant fuck all to him as he didn't even leave it a day before he went back on the pussy wagon. God, I'm starting to sound more like Lex. Talking of Lex, she is disgusted at Kyle's behavior, but I'm not with him anymore, I no longer have any rights to him.

I have been sitting with Derek and his friends for the rest of the week, they are so funny, that I have never laughed so much in a long time. Lex is starting to come around the whole Derek being ok. We haven't forgotten what he has done, but I guess everyone does deserve a second chance. Derek and I haven't done anything intimate apart from the hand holding on Tuesday. He hasn't pushed for anything or brought it up. He was being there for me and I appreciated it.

When I got downstairs ready to head to school with Lex, Mom and Dad are standing in the hallway looking at a letter. From the look on their faces, it's not good news. I do a little throat cough to show I am in the room. When they both look up at me, I see that look again, sadness, sympathy. Great just what I need on last day of school. No idea what I'm going to do this weekend, but I know I'm going to spend a lot of it away from this house.

"God, what now?" Yes, I sound more like a bitch, but I really can't help it.

"A letter came, it's about Caitlin's hearing," Mom says, waiting for me to break down at any second just hearing that name. I am not going to fall apart, I'm getting used to hearing her name, and I'm not going to give that power of myself to someone who isn't right in the head.

"What does it say?" I try to keep my voice calm, but I'm already starting to feel numb. It's becoming a normal defense mechanism to numb myself when bringing up Caitlin and that night. I had a nightmare again last night. I was back at the school dance.

I'm walking towards Kyle, looking at his handsome face smiling back at me. I was going to give him my intimate gift, my virginity. I'm walking closer and closer, but every step I take, Kyle never gets closer. I start to walk faster, I feel someone from behind me, and I try to run. I scream out Kyle's name, watching his face morph to shock and confusion, I know what happens next. I get stabbed twice from behind. When it happened, Caitlin was pulled back, but in my dream, she was holding onto my throat, sneering at me. She grabs my jaw and faces my face towards Kyle. I feel the tears fall down my cheeks. Caitlin is breathing so heavily, sneering at my tears.

"He was never yours. You deserved this. He doesn't want you, now you don't have him, ironic isn't it. You stayed by his side, yet where is here now?" I look up and surely Kyle is dancing in the middle of the dance floor, smiling at a different girl. Everyone around me doesn't acknowledge that I am in pain, I need their help.

"He never loved you, you know that, deep down you knew you two wouldn't last. Yet this was the outcome. This time I will make sure I end this..." I feel the knife start to slice my throat, and I wake up screaming bloody murder. I cried like I never cried before. It felt so real, I felt the knife against me, Caitlin's breath.

Mom and Dad came in, trying to hold me. At that moment, I needed them, more than anything. I cried into my mom's chest as she held me. My dad held me from behind stroking my hair. They stayed with me till I fell back to sleep. The look on their faces, I'm not surprised that they think I'm about to have an anxiety attack or something.

"She is pleading guilty to attempted murder, but she is playing it up as mental health problems, which means she may not go to jail but to a psychotic ward. The sentence may not be life. She's still not taking the blame for the photos, and the umm... the umm... dog thing," Mom says, trying to talk to me gently. Caitlin might not go to jail? I am suffering from nightmares, my life is no longer the same, and I'm no longer the sweet, shy girl I once was. This is all her fault, and yet she won't be punished like she deserves. My breath is picking up on how angry I am.

"You don't have to go to the hearing as she has pleaded guilty for hurting you. I think it's best you don't go, they don't need any more from you." Dad quickly adds in, I see them both try to walk towards me, but I don't want them. I put my hands up to show them I need them to stop. I hear Lex's car pull up so I grab my bag and run out of that house. I climb into Lex's car and tell her to drive. She looks at me and to my house, where my parents are standing at the door, watching me, least they aren't trying to stop me.

When we pull away I start to feel calmer, my breathing starts to slow down. I can tell Lex wants to know what happened, but glad she isn't pushing. I just need a moment to gather my thoughts. Caitlin getting away with what she has done, I still can't process it.

"Caitlin is blaming her mental life..." Lex doesn't say anything but stays quiet for me to continue. "There's a chance she won't go to jail, she will end up in a psychiatric ward, even that may not be for life." I look out the window, but I can feel the anger coming from Lex. I feel the same way, where the fuck is the justice?

"What the fucking hell? She is going to get away with almost killing you? This is so completely unfair, she deserves to be where the rest of the rapists and murderers are," Lex yells, hitting her steering wheel. I'm watching her, I'm wondering why aren't I hitting things? I raise my voice to my parents when they do my head in, but why aren't I showing this now?

"When is the hearing again?" Lex asks trying to calm down.

"Next Monday."

"Few days before Christmas? Are they sick? I didn't realize it was that soon, remember your parents talking about it, but it slipped through one ear and out the other.

"Yeah, they are starting to annoy me, to the point I hate going home. I'm starting to feel numb Lex. I feel all these emotions inside of me and it's the nasty, horrible ones I'm releasing. I don't feel like me anymore, it's scary. I'm resenting my parents. I gave up on Kyle. I almost pushed you away." I ramble on, and I feel Lex lean towards me and hugs me, and I hug her back.

"You have gone through a terrible ordeal, yes I sound like my grandmother saying that, but you have. Some people take years to get over almost dying. It's the shock of it all. Some people get PTSD. You will get back to your old self eventually."

"What if I don't? What happens if this is me now, forever?"

"Don't matter, I still love you, you will always have me. We will get through this together. If you ever need to rant, yell, throw things, I will be there. How many times have you been there where I have ranted about the dickheads I've dated? My turn to be there for you, you're my family." I feel the tears prickly behind my eyes by her words. Even if I stay as this shell of a person, I'm glad I know I have at least one person in my life I can rely on.

"I do love you," I say squeezing her tight, then letting go.

"I know, we are stuck with each other for life, bummer for you," Lex smiles at me, and I laugh in return. Lex helps me try and forget Caitlin and the letter. I just know when I'm alone with my thoughts, it will all come crashing down on me once again.

When we arrive at school, I feel calmer and relaxed. I link my arm through Lex's as we walk towards the entrance, but I stumble to a halt from what I see in front of me. Standing just a few feet away is Kyle, but that's not what has been frozen to stone, it's the girl pressed into his side, who he is smiling down at, Mrs. Long Legs. They look like a celebrity couple with how good they look together. I feel my heart is beating so fast, it's going to crash out of my chest any second. Lex looks where I'm staring and I can feel her anger roll out of her.

"Come on, you don't deserve this shit, I have no clue what that boy is thinking," Lex tries to pull me away, but I feel my feet are cemented to the floor. He has moved on already, I was that easy to get over. Everything Savannah said when she bullied me, my dreams with Caitlin. I never use to believe a word, but maybe I wasn't as special as I thought. "Come on," with that I follow Lex to her locker. We walk in silence, neither of us have any idea why Kyle is acting like this, and no words can explain it.

"Hey beautiful." I turn around to see Derek walking towards me, I give a small smile with a Hey back. "There's a party tonight at Toms, his parents are away this weekend, you guys fancy it?" I like that he isn't just asking me, he includes all of us. It's going to be the first Friday since I got better that I'm not doing something with Kyle, fair enough I have pulled Lex into being there for me the last few Fridays. It's because I knew it would be too awkward for me and Kyle being alone. I guess I do need to start breaking out of the old habit. I can't keep Lex away from James every Friday, it's not fair to her.

"Yeah, sounds good. What you think Lex?" I can feel Lex isn't 100 percent sure about this, but she knows that I probably need an excuse to get away from the Friday night tradition.

"Yeah, I will let James know."

"Cool, see you guys at lunch." Derek starts to walk away, but stops, then turns around and quickly kisses my cheek. I feel my cheeks blush by the contact. I have no idea what made him do it. I have no idea why I'm just standing there in shock. Derek waits for me to yell at him, but when I don't, he gives me a quick smile and walks away.

"What the Holy, Moses and Jesus, was that? I can't believe he kissed you, yeah it was your cheek, but still. What was that boy thinking?" Lex rambles on as we head to homeroom.

"No idea, I'm shocked as you, I wasn't expecting that," it's the truth. Part of me didn't mind it. It's a small part, but I wanted to be wanted. God did that even make sense?

"Well as long as that boy doesn't try any other moves on you. You just ended things with Kyle, you're not ready to jump into another relationship." I definitely wasn't ready for another relationship, but what if it didn't have to lead to a relationship?

eight

By the time lunch came around, everyone was talking about the party at Tom's. I didn't think I would be excited about it, but I was. This is the first party I got personally invited to. Lex and I were doing the whole girly thing, talking about what we were going to wear. We decided it had to be tight and sexy. I gave Lex a look, but she told me I had no choice. I was dragging her with me, and I had to do this for her, even though I don't remember forcing her once.

"I think I'm going to wear a red, tight dress that shows my best assets," Lex says licking her straw, staring at James, who looks like he wants to eat her. God I don't need to see this.

"What about you Ali? What you thinking of wearing?" Tom asks opposite me, staring at Lex, god men are easily distracted. Don't ask me why I say what I'm about to, but I have an urge to see the reaction.

"Hmm, I think I might wear a white dress, to show my innocence. But as its white, means I can't wear any underwear can I?" I look up to see all the guys looking at me now, with big eyes, not expecting me to say something like that. Even Lex is staring at me, giving me a smirk. "Yeah, my dress might be see through, but it will be dark, no one will see anything. Will they? There's always that saying, easy access, right?" With that, Derek starts choking on his drink. I can't help but smile, this is fun, no wonder why Lex does it. Just hope I can do it as good as her.

"Yeah, white sounds good, very virginal" Lex adds in giving me a wink.

"Yeah, seems fitting. Just think, I'm probably one of the only girls in school who is so tight..." I hear more coughing, trying so hard not to laugh, and look like this is a normal, boring conversation. " I mean uptight, I need to dress like the other girls, fit in more, just hope I don't get wet," again I hear the guys groan. "I heard Tom has a pool and doesn't want people to get my dress wet, I don't want to give people a little show do I?"

"Als, you know I'm tempted to get you wet now..." Lex says but gets interrupted by all the guys with moans and groans.

"Ok we get your point, stop with the dirty talk, or I'm going to have to wank off right here in the cafeteria. You, women, are evil," Tom says, and Lex and I giggle.

"Sorry, Lex started it," yes that did sound childish but I love the silliness that is happening between us.

"What? Don't blame me. You started going on about being tight and wet." Lex whines at me.

"You started with the whole tight red dress thing sucking on your straw, all the guys were perving at you."

"Hey," all the guys complained.

"You guys were, you all have dirty thoughts."

"We weren't talking about wearing no panties, and getting wet," Simon next to Tom says. I started laughing but stopped when I feel the hairs on the back of my neck stand up. I know who is behind me, I don't want to turn around, but my body betrays me and turns. When I look up, I see Kyle looking down at me, with hunger and anger in his eyes. Why is he looking at me like that? Not my fault he came at the wrong time to hear what Simon said.

I notice that Mrs. Long Legs walk towards him, I look at Kyle and raise my eyebrow to say what? You can't judge me, with that whore at your side. Well hoping that is what I'm putting across. He grunts then walks off to his table with Mrs. LL at his heels.

"God that was awkward, bad timing for him to hear about you not wearing panties thing," Tom says.

"Yeah, bad timing, but not my fault," I say, shrugging my shoulders.

"You ok? Derek and Lex ask at the same time, I nod and try and give them a reassuring smile.

"Yeah, he probably thinks we got you all wet, as you aren't wearing your panties. It's my charm that does it, don't blame him for looking angry. I am a woman's man," Tom says and we all burst out laughing. God I love Tom.

I feel eyes on me and when I look over to Kyle, I see him staring at me. I can't look away. I feel my body start to heat up. Why is he looking at me like that? I start to feel that ache build up. I cross my legs together trying to dull the ache. I need to look away, but I can't. I feel that electricity flow through us both, drawing us together. All too soon, it's broken when I see Mrs. LL kiss Kyle on the cheek. Kyle winced knowing I'm looking, when he looks back at me, I look away. Derek did the same thing to me this morning, but I know what she's after. Kyle between her legs, I know he will be.

The last class today was gym and I could not be bothered with it. I just want to go home and get ready for the party. I keep thinking what am I going to wear. I have got a white dress but don't have the nerve to go without wearing panties, it's not like any of the guys at the table are going to try and have a peek. Will they? Oh god, hope not. I don't have Lex with me in this class, she is in a different group, which I completely hate. I'm always on my own, and I always feel the annoyance if someone is forced to partner with me.

I am a runner, but my hand and eye coordination is non-existent. I leave the locker room and enter the gym, and sit on the bleachers with the rest of the class. I sit on my own and just sit with my thoughts, normally I don't mind, but these days my thoughts aren't pleasant. I'm trying really hard to just think of the party, and what this one will be like, but then I can't help but overhear some girls talking about Kyle a few rows down from me, obviously not realizing I'm nearby.

"Well Stacey, told me, that Kerry told her, that Kyle is back on the market. I didn't believe it at first, as rumors can be a letdown, but I saw it with my own eyes. He's back to his old ways," Blonde number 1 says squealing at blonde number 2.

"Not surprised. Men like him don't change. He's hot, he can have any girl he wants, why would he want to settle down? Especially with that goody-goody?"

"I know right? Bet she's still a virgin, you can tell by how she acts. Plus she got stabbed, you don't need that kind of baggage in your life," Blonde number 1 says. I can't help but feel anger at them at being so insensitive, it's taking all my control, to just sit and not punch them in the throat.

"Yeah, Kyle doesn't seem the type to want that kind of shit on his shoulders. He's that aloof, not wanting baggage type. Think I may get a bit of that action at the party tonight?" Stay calm, just breathe, he's not yours. Who cares what they are saying? I keep saying over and over in my head.

"We should offer him a threesome, so he can't say no, I wouldn't mind sharing with you. You are my best friend after all."

"That's so sweet, yeah, don't want him looking elsewhere. To-night he is ours." Blonde 1 and 2 squeal and I feel that my ears are bleeding. I have the image of Kyle and these idiots at it in my head.

"Alison McCartney, you're team B," Coach Watson yells, bring-ing me out on my kill lazar stare at the blonde twins. I hear them gasp when they hear me stand up few rows behind them.

I start to walk down and can't help but want to offload some of this anger. I need to let some of this out or I'm going to snap. I know I'm just going to walk away, try and not let it get to me, but they are talking about me being stabbed as it was an inconvenience to the person who was meant to be my best friend, my boyfriend. How dare they say such shit, about something they don't even understand. I am so tempted to just give them a piece of my mind but know I will cause a scene.

"Hey don't let those girls get to you, heard what they were saying. They are just slutty whores." I turn around to see Savannah standing beside me staring at the girls, who are looking elsewhere but at us. I haven't spoken to Savannah since she defended me from Trina. "They are that desperate, they are going to offer both of themselves, as they are afraid he will turn them down. They wouldn't have suggested it if they were certain he would say yes." I know she is trying to make me feel better, but it's the thing that he is going to bed one or both of them.

"I know, me and Kyle aren't together anymore. It's not a nice image to see in my head, them having their wicked way with him," I shiver trying not to think about it.

"It's hard, moving on. I get it. But this is the thing you have to get used to, women talking like that about Kyle. Surprised you never heard girls talk about him before, but you were always in your little bubble when it came to him. No, offense." I look at Savannah to see that she isn't being mean just honest. Was I that into Kyle I blocked out what girls said about him? Was I just lucky that I never had the chance to hear it? I heard the odd thing from Savannah when she brought stuff up, but I always ignored it. I never let it sink in. Have no idea why?

"Yeah I guess I didn't want it to affect how I felt for him. I just ignored it, pretended it wasn't a big deal."

"What's changed?" God good question.

"Me, I have changed. I think my innocent, naive little head, is no longer innocent. I see all the dark, as before I just saw all light."

"Very profound. Just try and not let this get you down. You're better than that," Savannah says watching Couch yelling girl's names, telling them which group they will be in.

"Why you being so nice to me? You use to make my life hell?" I had to ask, it's been bugging me, think now is better than ever to get it out.

"You almost died. I know I bullied you, I know it wasn't right, but you didn't deserve to die. I may have made threats that you shouldn't be here, but it was all talk, it was me being a grade A bitch, but wouldn't want it to actually happen. The reasons for my bullying, hmm... guess it was 'cause I was kind of jealous," Savannah says with a shrug and I gape at her. Her jealous of me? She is rich, popular, wanted by most guys in school, why would she be jealous of me?

"Why were you jealous of me, I have nothing to be jealous of."

"You had Kyle and Lex, following you as you were their queen when we were kids, you didn't have to do anything but smile at them, and they would do anything you wanted. Me, I had to be mean to get my friends to do what I wanted, yes it's childish but at that time, I wanted to be queen to my friends. You were turning into this really pretty girl. You don't even try, you tried at nothing and yet it all fell into place for you. You changed your clothes when I started being mean, wearing clothes that were way too big for you. So thought if I kept at it, going on and on about Kyle, you would leave him too. I wanted Kyle, but not for the right reasons. I wanted him to be at my side, looking at me like he looked at you. No one noticed the stares you both gave each other, but I did. I wanted to be you, I kept that anger that I wasn't, on you. Sounds so stupid saying it all out, but in my head, it's what kept me going, what kept me torturing you," Savannah sighs as she spewed out the whole truth.

"I can't believe it. I thought you had the perfect life, you look amazing, every guy wants you, you're rich, and you have so many friends." It's hard to digest this. Savannah wanted to be me.

"I have to work hard to look like this, with no makeup, I look pale, with bags under my eyes. I look unhealthy, you look pretty and it's all natural. The clothes I wear I make sure it shows off my assets as I have hardly any curves, and I'm a little on the skinny side. Guys want me so they can fuck me. The people who follow me, they aren't really my friends, they just want to be, part of the in crowd. Deep down, my life is fake. That's why I was jealous of you. You aren't fake, neither is your life." Oh God, I didn't even once question Savannah's life. She has the same issues as me. Wanting to be wanted and noticed, Savannah just went the wrong way about it.

"Thank you for telling me all of this, you have no idea, how this has changed things. I was always insecure about my body, my life, even my friends. But guess I had it better than I thought.

"Yeah, I didn't think what went on with your life either, I just thought your life looked easy, but you never know what goes on in the background, do you?"

"Guess not."

"Truce then? Do you forgive me?" I look at Savannah and know, that I have. I feel closure from my past insecurities. Just need to deal with these new insecurities.

"Yeah, truce." I shake Savannah's hand and we both smile at each other.

"Alison, Savannah, stop giving each other the googly eyes and join your groups, the match is about to start. Savannah and I giggle and join the rest of our group.

nine

L ex drove to her house and packed a bag, well when I say bag I mean, a suitcase, of clothes, shoes, and makeup options. I waited patiently in the car as wasn't in the mood to see Lex's parents, and see all the pity and sympathy from them as well. Lex's parents Tracey and Aiden Carter are both amazing parents, they are like my second family on how many times I spent over at Lex's over the years. But they are acting like what my parents do around me, fuss over everything I do and say. I love them, but if I can't handle my own parents doing it, then not going to handle another's parents doing the same thing.

When Lex puts her suitcase in the trunk, I roll my eyes thinking that it looks like she's planning on running away then getting ready at my house for the party. I asked Lex if she could help me get ready as had no clue what to wear, she even offered to do my hair and makeup. I jumped at the chance not having to do it myself. I love my hair being played with. When Lex and I were kids, we use to play hairdressers. Lex was normally the hairdresser as she was more girly than me, but I loved the feeling of someone playing with my hair, I found it really soothing.

"God you moving out? Looks like you took everything you own," I say to Lex when she jumps into her seat.

"Trust me if I was moving out I will have ten times the luggage. I brought clothes for you to try on to and shoes to match the outfits, was making sure I came prepared." I can't help but roll my eyes.

"Well most of your clothes accentuate your cleavage, my boobs aren't as huge as yours."

"Stop whining, wait till we get to yours and see what I have. You are judging and complaining before you even see what I brought. Plus your boobs are a good handful, most girls would kill to have your goods."

"Most girls want yours," I say which is true, girls always want bigger.

"Yeah, but they are a pain. I get back pain at times because they are that big, I have to go to certain stores to get bras, as most places don't have my size."

"I didn't realize, they look good though."

"Yeah that's the only positive thing, they look good to look at. James loves them, but what guy wouldn't? Just a pain at times. Guess we are never happy with what we have got huh?" God ain't that the truth.

"Yeah, every girl wants better, than what they have."

"Being a girl sucks at times. Boys just have to put on a T-shirt, jeans, mess their hair up a little and that's them done. They don't realize how good they got it."

"Yeah, we have to handle periods, and childbirth. They don't have to worry about all that. You can tell God was a guy. He made us women suffer through everything," I say, sighing on why couldn't God be a woman.

"Yeah, we should write a complaint letter to God," Lex suggest and I can't help but giggle on where this conversation is going.

"We should. Dear God, it's unfair us women have to go through periods, and childbirth. Men should suffer something too..."

"Don't forget the pain we go through when losing your virginity.

Why can't it hurt men too?"

"Oh yeah PS, they should experience pains when losing their virginity too. Yours sincerely Alison and Lexi. What you think?"

"Perfect, we just need to write it down and post it to Heaven," we both burst out laughing on how stupid we sound.

"It's true though us women got the wrong end of things."

"Bet that's what you say to James." Lex gasps and punches my arm. We burst out laughing again. Can already feel that tonight is going to be a good night.

My room looks like a bomb hit it. Clothes are everywhere. I tried on nearly everything Lex has chucked at me, but nothing looked right. I told Lex I wanted to look sexy, but comfortable, and most of Lex's dresses were too revealing on the boob part. My boobs aren't as big as Lex's, the necklines droop a little more than if she wore them. I decided to wear the white dress, and Lex approved screaming that the guys at the table are going to be second-guessing all night if I'm wearing panties or not. Lex threw me a white G-string saying it's underwear, but no one will be able to tell that I'm wearing any. I hold it up, and it looks like dental floss. But I put them on. I'm wearing a white, lace, strapless bra. The dress is strapless, and I wouldn't feel right going without a bra on.

"You look so hot, every guy is going to be drooling over you tonight," Lex says from behind me. I look at her and she has decided on a tight black dress. Her boobs are pushed up and the material just covers her bum. I hope James stands behind her most of the evening or she's going to be given some guys a peek.

"You look super-hot, but don't you think its little short?" Lex waves me off giving me a pfft.

"I'm young, this is the only time in my life I can get away with this before I need to settle down." Guess she's right. Seize the day right? "Plus it doesn't help I'm not wearing any panties, don't tell James, it's a surprise." I can't help but scrunch up my face, all I know now is Lex is going commando to a very public party.

"Why did you have to share that bit of information?" I shiver then go to my closet to get my white sandal heels to go with my dress.

"Love to torture you." When I put my sandals on, I grab my purse and keys and look in the mirror one last time. My hair is down in waves, which Lex has perfected. My makeup looks all natural, not too much. Lex definitely should look into being a makeup artist, the girl has skill, but know she is adamant about being a nurse.

"Yeah noticed. You ready?" As I open my bedroom door, indicating I'm ready.

"Ready as I will ever be, come on sweets." Lex follows me down the stairs, Mom and Dad stand up from the couch to walk over to us.

"Oh, my mother of all things holy. What are you girls wearing?" My dad asks, and I can't help but roll my eyes. He really needs to learn to deal with me dressing like this. It's not like I will dress like this during the day, or to school. I know people will definitely stare if I walked into school wearing this.

"Honey, they look like any seventeen-year-old girl would. They look sexy," Mom chides in, trying to calm him down, but his eyes have bulged out.

Exactly, sexy. Which means every guy is going to be thinking that. God going to have a heart attack, can feel it coming." My dad puts his hand over his heart, I can't help but sigh at his dramatics, and Lex is trying not to laugh.

"Gerald stop being such a drama queen. You girls have fun and be careful." I look at my mom and wait for the worry talks about what could happen, and the what ifs, but none of it comes, I can't help but feel relieved.

"Thanks, mom, see you in the morning." I hear Dad groan again, I can't help but let slip a giggle as I walk out the door, when the door closes, Lex bursts out in a fit of laughter. I can't help but join.

"God your Dad is so hilarious. My dad is used to what I wear so he doesn't bat an eye, but your Dad, oh God. It's like he was trying for an Academy Award." Lex says holding her stomach trying to calm down before getting in her car. James is meeting us there, he promised some of his friends a game of bowling before the party. Guy's thing.

"Yeah, my dad has started acting all dramatic when he sees some of the outfits I wear. I swear most of them are really modest, compared to what most girls wear at school. Think he will have a heart attack if he ever stood in the hallway on a Friday.

"Yeah could imagine his eyes, popping out of his sockets. It's nice though that he cares, even though he did go over the top a little bit."

"Just a little?" We both burst out laughing again as Lex drives out heading towards Tom's house.

"Look at us, going to parties. Time has flown by. Next week is last week of school for Christmas, then few months left then that's it, no more high school." Lex says. I can't help but think how much has changed in such a short amount of time. I can't believe the year is almost over.

"I know, but part of me can't wait to move on to the next chapter in my life. Put all this behind me and think of the future. Least I know I got you, all the way through."

"Yeah, you are stuck with me. Just scary thinking about college. Bigger school, new people. Starting fresh." That's what is so appealing to me. No one will know who I am, and what I went through. I can't bloody wait.

"Yeah, think I will re-invent myself at college. Party more, maybe even date more. Hopefully, I will be ready to move on by then. See what good looking guys are lurking in those dorm rooms," I waggle my eyebrows at Lex causing her to laugh.

"Yeah, can imagine you going at it, on a desk, following your dirty desires." Lex giggles. I can't help but think of the time Kyle picked me up on his desk and touching me, pleasuring me. I start to feel the ache build between my legs just remembering rubbing myself against my hand as I touched him. I shake my head and try and clear my thoughts away from Kyle.

We talk about Christmas and organizing a day to the mall to get our presents in, and our future in college. When we pull up to Tom's house, I tell myself to have fun and enjoy it. I want some happy memories of high school, so I'm going to dance my butt off, maybe even have a few drinks. Never really drank alcohol, but I know I have Lex, who is the designated driver, so she will keep an eye on me.

ten

Entering Tom's house is like the last two parties I went to, crowded and loud. I take a deep breath and I follow Lex and walk towards the back of the house. This party is more X-rated than the last two as I'm sure I've seen a guy get a blow job, right in the open, and a guy feeling up a girl against the wall. I am definitely out of my depth here. When Lex opens a door that leads us outside, I never felt more relieved in my life. Outside is crowded but not as bad as inside, and no one seems to be doing anything sexual.

"What the fuck kind of party is this?" Lex asks taking my hand and guiding us to a bar opposite the pool. Does every house have a bar outside?

"I have no clue, but I'm definitely too innocent for this. I've seen a guy get sucked off in front of everyone, it's so demeaning. Don't know how the girl can do it, and not give a damn."

"We will stay out here, come on let's dangle our feet in the pool," Lex grabs two cans of Coke and guides us to a side of the pool away from everyone else. Right now, I'm not complaining.

"You seen James yet?" I ask.

"No, but going to text him we are outside. Hate that he might see what's going on inside. I may be adventurous, but I would never do half the shit that was going on in there." Lex points at the doors to the house. Least I know I'm not the only one who is a little disturbed by the shit that's going on. Does Tom know about this? Oh my God, what if it's that kind of party?

"What if it's a sex party or something? I will walk back home before I get involved in any of this."

"Calm down, it's not a sex party, some parties are just more out of control than others. Use to hear all sorts, so don't worry no one is going to make you do anything." I feel calmer already. I know Lex would make sure I stay safe anyway.

Lex and I stay in our spots, talking and laughing. When James arrives, he sits with us, happy to just chill. I feel happy and normal, experiencing a party with my best friend, even though we decided we didn't want to go back inside, I was happy with that.

"Hay gorgeous people. Anyone want a shot?" I turn to see Tom with a tray in his hands with loads of shots, many of different colors. Should I try one? Never had a shot before.

"No thanks, we're good Tom," Lex says.

"You sure?"

"I'll have one please," I quickly shout out, I realize I may have said that too quickly.

"You don't drink Als, you sure about this?"

"Yeah, want to give it a try." Was going to say you only live once, but held my tongue. Don't think Lex would appreciate that saying. I take the shot off Tom, it's a green and yellow colored, and I quickly down it. It burns my throat a little, but it tastes alright, not as bad as I thought it would be.

"One more?" I nod and he gives me another, this one is red, that one did burn, but it left a warm tingle down my throat.

"Thanks, Tom." I hand him the empty shot glasses back.

"No probs, see you guys later" Tom walks off to the next group, handing out the shots. I feel fine, nothing different. Maybe they aren't that strong.

"You ok?" Lex asks I roll my eyes. Just had two shots, not going to be suddenly shitfaced.

"Yeah, didn't taste that bad. I'm going to quickly head in, to use the toilet. Be right back." I stand up, righting my dress.

"Want me to come with? Know how chaotic it is in there."

"I will be fine, you guys can have a quick make out session till I get back," I wink at Lex, Lex laughs at me. "I'll be quick," I tell her and walk inside the house.

I feel all the heat as soon as I walk inside. I'm glad I'm wearing this dress, or I would be sweating loads. I squeeze through everyone till I see the stairs and start walking up. I try and keep my eyes focused on the stairs and not anywhere else, never know what my innocent eyes may see. I go down the hallway and see a line, is this for the toilets?

"Hi is this line for the bathroom?" I ask a girl who is also waiting.

"Yeah, it's taking bloody forever. Wish there was more than one," the girl sighs, and I can't help but sigh too. I quickly text Lex that the line is massive and I may be awhile. I lean against the wall. God this is going to take forever.

"Fancy a drink as you wait?" I hear Derek say. I turn my head to see him walking down the hallway.

"Yeah, sure. This line hasn't moved since I've been here." I take the red cup from Derek. I look inside and see it's beer. I take a sip, it has a horrible aftertaste but hope I get used to it.

"Hope no one is having sex in there," Derek says, drinking from his own cup.

"Ewww, that's gross. Who would have sex in the bathroom?"

"You would be surprised. So you enjoying yourself?"

"Yeah, but some things I will never be able to take back. I've seen some couples who aren't afraid of public affection if you know what I mean." Derek starts to laugh.

"Some parties are more out of control than others. Tonight must be one of them."

"That's what Lex said, well the some parties are more out of control than others. I could never be that kind of girl."

"That's what makes you one of a kind. It's nice seeing your innocence. It's what drew me to you. You would be a prize on any guys arm. You're the girl guys want to show off, introduce the parents too, etc." Wow, what do you say to that? "I know I messed things up, I let my personal pressures make me do something stupid, but hope we can still be friends. You are still important me. I will always care about you."

"I don't know what to say to that. You did hurt me, but I have been through worse since then. I would love us to be friends. You are one of the people I can relax around. You put me at ease. My parents treat me like a baby. You treat me like an adult, I appreciate that."

"Well, you know I'm always here if you ever need to talk, about anything."

"I appreciate that." I look at Derek and I see the guy that I did fall for before he started changing to a dominant ass.

"You're next." Derek points at the bathroom door. I didn't see the line go down.

"Didn't even notice the line was moving down. You really are a good distraction." Derek smiles at me. I quickly down the rest of my drink and head into the bathroom when the girl who was in front of me comes out.

I quickly relieve myself and check my reflection in her mirror, I look a little flush, but my makeover still looks fine. I don't even know why I'm checking myself out, but don't want to look like a slob, that's what I tell myself anyway. When I exit the bathroom, Derek is leaning against the opposite wall, when he sees me walk out, he gives me a big smile, and I can't help but smile back.

"You really have a great smile, you know that?" Derek says, stepping towards me and puts his arm out for me to link. Which I happily do.

"Thanks, very gentlemanly of you."

"Yeah, I have my moments." We start to walk down the hallway, towards the stairs, when I see a door slightly open, and I see Kyle standing there. I stop, and Derek looks at me with confusion, but I can't speak, I can't move.

I see a girl with blonde hair, walk seductively towards Kyle and glide her hands up his chest. I need to move away, I don't want to see this, but my body won't move. I can feel Derek behind me, trying to guide me away, but I still don't move. The girl starts to unbutton his shirt, very slowly, and he just stands there looking down at her. I can't see his face to see what he's thinking. Is he looking at her like he used to look at me? I can feel my heart beating erratically that it feels it's going to bounce out of my chest. I can feel the tears prickle behind my eyes.

"Come on, you don't need to see this," Derek says, grabbing onto my arm, trying to pull me away, gently as possible. But I can't move. The girl has finished unbuttoning his shirt and helps roll it off. He's standing there, topless, her hands feel his abs, touching what was once mine.

"Alison, please," Derek says a bit loudly that causes Kyle to turn towards the voice, when he sees me, I see shock, guilt and sadness in his eyes. I feel the first tear fall. The girl doesn't pay attention to us and starts to unbutton his jeans, that's when my body finally moves, not able to take in the image anymore.

"Come on." Derek guides me into the kitchen, I feel my happy mood has died in that hallway. I knew Kyle has moved on, it didn't take him long. I suspected he was sleeping around again, but to see it, it's a completely different thing. "Here drink this." Derek gives me a shot of something.

"What is it?" I smell it and cringe.

"Something that will help numb the pain." I watch Derek drink his, and I do the same, feeling the harsh burn slide down my throat. Definitely stronger than what Tom was giving me.

"Have another, it will help." Derek pours more into our shot glasses. I drink it. Derek and I, take few more shots to the point, where I start to feel that happy buzz again.

"Where the fuck have you been?" Lex yells at me, I stumble into the counter, by the shock. Ow, that hurt. "You drunk?"

"What, no... I had few shots, to help me." I say, trying to stand still, but my body keeps swaying a little. Why is my body swaying? Weird.

"Help you with what? You were meant to come back after you used the bathroom. What's happened?" Lex says grabbing onto my arms, trying to get answers from me. My head feels so fuzzy, it's taking a little longer to process what she's asking.

"She saw Kyle with another girl," Derek says from my side. Why doesn't he seem drunk?

"What you saw Kyle having sex with someone else?" Lex looks shocked and disgusted.

"No, but the stripping bit, she seemed like she was going to cry, so I gave her few shots to help ease the pain. Thought I was doing a good thing. She shouldn't shed another tear for that shithead," Derek says and I laugh at the word shit head.

"You should have brought her to me, but least she's not upset, well for now anyway. Going to take her home. Come on Als." Lex links onto my arm and starts to pull me away from the kitchen.

"Wait," I yell out and stumble over to Derek. I throw my arms around his neck and give him a hug. "Thank you for looking after me." I kiss his cheek and step back to Lex, who looks a little put out by the move, but I don't care. Derek made me happy again. He made me feel better. I forgot all about Kyle and what I saw, I even forgot all the shit that has been playing around in my head.

"Come on sweetie, home for you." Lex guides me to her car and helps me get in.

"Love you, Lex, hope you're not angry with me," I slur a little. God it's a little hard, getting my words out. I start to feel little sleepy too.

"Never angry at you. Just be careful with Derek though. Something about him I don't like." I feel my eyes getting heavy, and I start to drift off.

"He's just my nice friend, still love Kyle." I then let the darkness in and fall into a deep sleep.

eleven

I feel like someone came into my room last night and punched my skull over and over. This is what a hangover feels like. Why do people drink every weekend to feel like this the following day? I have to suck my mouth few times to build up some saliva, as my mouth is completely dry. God I feel like crap, don't even want to know what I look like. I sit up and my head hurts so much, I can feel the pulse thumping. I look down at myself and see I'm only in my underwear, my dress is on the floor with my shoes, must have just stripped down and fell into bed last night. I grab my robe and head to the bathroom. I need to pee like there's no tomorrow.

When I finally do see myself in the mirror, I look just like how I feel. I have black panda eyes, eye shadow is smeared all over my face. I get a facial wipe and clean my face, then run the shower. I smell like stale beer, and I only had one cup. When I let the water flow over me, I lean my head against the cold tiles. Last night's event run through my head. Watching Kyle get stripped by another girl, was definitely the worst things I could experience. I got stabbed, but watching that with Kyle was like being stabbed all over again, but to my heart.

I remember Derek making me laugh, trying to get me away from witnessing Kyle and that girl. He was there for me. I'm starting to rely on him, and I don't know how I feel about that. I remember why I liked him in the first place, but he started to change, and the whole Savannah thing. I feel so confused. He hasn't pushed me for anything, he hasn't even tried it on with me. He's just been there. Right now, I don't know what I would be like without him.

When I go downstairs to get a drink, my parents are in the kitchen, whispering to each other, when they see me, they stop talking. Great, they were talking about me. I go the fridge and grab some apple juice, I have two glasses. I feel my body start to feel better.

"Thirsty?" Mom asks.

"Yeah," I say, and put my glass in the dishwasher. I start to leave, but my dad asks me to sit down. What now?

"What's up?" I ask.

"We are worried about you. We heard you come home last night. We can tell you were drinking. You never drink." Dad says, I can't help but roll my eyes.

"Most people my age drink at parties. Kyle drinks at parties. I had a few. I'm young I wanted to experience it."

"Yeah, maybe other kids drink, but they aren't my child. I don't want you going out, drinking to the point you are banging into a piece of furniture on the way to your room."

"It was my first time drinking. If I want to drink again, I will. I felt happy, everything wrong in my life faded away. As I said, if I want to drink I will." I say matter of factly, what can they do?

"Young lady, if you live under our roof, you will obey our rules, this may sound cliché, but that's how it is." They did not go old school on me?

"Fine, I will just move out then. Is that what you want? I only come here to eat and sleep. I don't mind leaving if that's what you want." I love my parents but hate this house anyway. My head keeps thumping every two seconds, Can't think straight.

"Gerald!" Mom grabs onto my dad's arm, afraid I will actually leave.

"You wouldn't leave, you have nowhere to go," Dad says, his voice starting to rise.

"Watch me." I give a pointed look that I'm serious.

"Think this is getting too far, Gerald, she isn't leaving her home."

"She won't leave. This is her home. We need to start setting boundaries." Dad says, I feel my anger start to rise up in me. I drink once. This is what I get. I don't do anything wrong, ever!

"You kidding me. Set boundaries. I drank once, once! I am a straight A student. I did all the work I missed when I was healing from being stabbed twice. I'm still ahead of most students in my class. You act like I'm a terror. If I'm that much of a burden, maybe I should leave. I will. Trust me."

"Gerald, don't let my baby leave," Mom cries. I feel bad that I'm hurting her, but I'm not being talked to like I am a horrible child when there're people who are worse. I still haven't done anything wrong.

"Look what you're doing to your mother. You don't talk to us. You run for hours on end. You don't really eat. You have nightmares, it's not healthy. You need to speak to someone if you aren't willing to speak to us." A therapist? Really?

"What I'm doing to my mother? You're the one giving me an ultimatum, just because I drank once. ONCE! I ALMOST DIED! You forgot that? It's going to take time for me to get over that. Sorry, I'm not the goody-goody daughter, you once loved. I'm sorry six weeks later, I'm still not over it. Bloody sue me. I will leave, I will not look back if that's what you want. You want me to leave? DO YOU?" My anger is seething through, I can't stop it. My head is banging even more, but I don't care.

"NO! We don't want you to leave. You're right, we need to give you time. We don't want you to leave. Do we Gerald?" Mom says in tears.

"Love..."

"Do we Gerald?" Mom says sternly to Dad.

"Right, we would never want you to leave. Just be careful about the things you do. Remember the consequences." Dad says before standing up and walking away. I stand up and walk away too. I need to get rid of this built up anger, I still have boiling in me. How dare he talk to me like this? One thing, one thing, I did wrong I almost get kicked out. I am going to drink again. Out of stubbornness and because I was happy, and my head was empty. No Caitlin, No Kyle. Nothing.

"Honey, please." Mom begs me.

"Going for a run, see you later." I walk out the door and start a slow jog away from the house I grew up in. My head hurts, but I ignore it. I keep going till my head goes blank, I start to feel numb. I see the image of Kyle and the girl in my head, start to flow away. I start to feel guilt on how I'm treating my parents. How I spoke to my dad. I know I'm hurting them emotionally. I let it all slide out of my head. I can't handle all the different emotions running through me anymore.

When I get back home, I am physically and emotionally exhausted. I walk upstairs, not even looking if my parents are about. I think I have sweated out my hangover. I have another shower and lie on my bed, staring at the ceiling. I hear my phone buzz on my desk, I walk over to it and find I have a few text messages from Lex and Derek.

Lex: How you feeling?

Lex: Take it you're still sleeping it off, txt me when you get this x x

Lex: Hope you're not ignoring me young lady x x

Lex: If you don't txt me back soon, will drive to your house, don't think I won't x x

Derek Hope you're feeling ok. I shouldn't have given you all those shots. But if you're up to it, there's a party at McKenna's.

Can pick you up if you want? x

I look at the message from Derek and decide why not. I know if I don't go, I will be spending another night in. I don't want my parents trying to talk to me again, especially Dad, not in the mood to talk about how me doing one normal teenage thing makes me a delinquent. I quickly reply back to Derek telling him to pick me up at 8. I reply back to Lex.

Me: Sorry, felt rough this morning. Parents decided that I'm a trouble maker, from one night of me acting like a normal teenager. I went for a run, just getting back now x x

I wait for a reply which I get few minutes later.

Lex: You're a newbie at drinking, those shots were going to make you feel rough. Sorry about your parents x x

Me: Me and Dad really went at it. That bad, I almost got kicked out x x

Lex: Surely it wasn't that bad ??????

Me: It was that bad, Mom had to calm him down. He over exaggerated the situation, and me drinking last night. He always over exaggerates, doing my head in x x x

Lex: Blimey, they knew you were drinking?

Me: Yeah, wasn't as quiet as I thought x x

Lex: LOL well got a date night with James, txt me tomorrow, love you. Hope you and parents sort things out x x

Me: We will see, have fun x x

Lex: I plan to ;) love you x x

Me: Love you too x x

I don't know why I didn't mention Derek, and the party I'm going to with him, but I know deep down why I didn't. I knew she would try and talk me out of it, or go on and on about Derek trying to get back with me or something. If he wanted to get together with me, he would have done it by now. I go through my closet and try and find something nice to wear. I don't want to give the wrong impression to Derek, but still want to make an effort. It's another party I've been invited to, this time Lex won't be there. I'm sure I will be fine.

I decide to catch up on some reading on my Kindle as I wait to start getting ready. I started to read a stepbrother romance by Sabrina Paige, and it's a little addicting. I wish I had the spunk Katherine had, she reminds so much like Lex at times. I don't know how she didn't cave sooner, Caulter is drool-worthy. When it was time to get ready, I decide to wear black leather mini skirt, white top that hangs from one shoulder, and my black suede knee high boots. I back comb my hair, giving it a messy, wavy look, I see Lex do it all the time. I don't think I did a bad job. I wear brown eye shadow and clear lip gloss, don't want to overdo it. I look in the mirror, and wow, think I look hot. Never thought I would say that about myself, but I do.

I walk downstairs, deciding to sit on my swing as I wait for Derek, don't want him meeting my parents. I know they will interrogate him, asking a million questions. The mood Dad's in, I wouldn't be surprised if he slammed the door in his face, especially since they know what he did with Savannah. When I get to the door, I hear Dad yell out to me.

"Where do you think you're going?" Dad says as he stands up from the couch, with Mom walking behind him.

"Out with a friend." I turn to leave, but Dad obviously isn't finished yet.

"After last night, I don't think so. Especially not dressed like that," Dad points his finger up down at my outfit, I roll my eyes at him.

"I'm dressed fine, I'm not staying in this house for another minute. I'm going mad staying in my room. I'm going out to see some friends and have a laugh."

"You don't have many friends," Dad says, and I feel like he just punched me in the stomach.

"Gerald," Mom scolds my dad, giving him an angry look.

"That's not what I meant." Dad looks at the ground and I feel like I just want to punch him and cry.

"Yeah, I don't have many friends, but I do have some, maybe not loads like the other kids. I'm going to this party. If you try and stop me, I will pack a bag and leave this house, if this is how you're going to start treating me, when I get invites out. Now that people want to hang with me, you have a problem?" I stay tight lipped, I feel the tears build up again. Why do I feel like I'm crying so much these days?

"Honey, go meet with your friends will see you in the morning," Mom says pulling Dad away, not gently either.

"Bye," I say over my shoulder, as I quickly run out the door and to my swing, Derek still not here yet. I sit on the swing and start to push myself a little. I let the breeze glide through me, calming me. When I start to feel my body, relax. I feel the heat run through my body, I know that someone is near me. I know by how my body is reacting to who it is. Kyle.

twelve

"What you want Kyle?" I ask, not turning around, I hear him walk towards me. He starts to push me on the swing.

"Saw you run out of the house, wanted to see if you're ok," Kyle says, sounding concerned. He has no right to be concerned for me anymore. Especially what I saw last night. It's starting to be a pattern with me seeing him in the awkward situations at parties.

"You don't need to worry about me anymore. I'm fine, I'm getting there."

"We may not be talking anymore, but I'm always going to care for you." Yeah, he knows how to show it.

"Don't Kyle. Don't try and act that you care for me, if you did you wouldn't have moved on so quickly. I see all these girls all over you, stripping you, and it took you what? A couple of days to move on? Getting back to your old ways." I raise my voice. I stop the swing and get off, turning to stare at him, showing my anger towards him.

"I'm trying to move on from you, you ended it with me remember. I'm trying to move on from you Als." Kyle walks up to me, glaring down at me.

"I ended it because you rather cozy up with other girls than your own girlfriend, your supposedly best friend. How would you feel if I started slutting myself out to other guys? How you are with other girls? I might let a guy strip me down at a party, what you think? Going to a party tonight, might even do what the girls do at some of these parties." I glare back. I feel my breath coming heavily on how angry I am at him. How my dad treated me before. I'm letting it all come out.

"Don't you fucking dare say that shit to me? You are a good girl, you're innocent, you aren't like those girls. Don't try and make me jealous." How self-involved is he that I would do this for him. I was just proving how hurtful it is to see someone move on so quickly.

"If I did it, I would be doing it for me, not you, you ass. You're moving on, so will I. I'm no longer the goody-goody. I am no longer that person. I don't even know who the fuck I am, but if I want to have fun, if that includes other guys, then so what?"

"Shut up," Kyle seethes at me.

"Why? I might let another guy touch me, feel..." I don't get a chance to let another word out, as Kyle's lips slam down on mine. It takes me a few seconds to click on what's happening. I do a little jump and wrap my legs around him. He pushes me against the tree, grinding himself against me. I can't help the moan that leaves my mouth. This feels so good. All my anger evaporates. All I feel is want, need, a release.

I grab onto Kyle's hair, guiding his face harder against me. Letting his lips, dominate mine. My skirt rides up to my waist. I feel Kyle's denim jeans pressing against me. I'm panting at how much I needed this. Kyle's fingers start to slide in my underwear till he feels my clit, he starts rubbing, making my legs start to shake. I use all my power to keep my legs in a tight grip. I lean my head against the tree. Kyle adds couple fingers and start to glide it in and out of me, going faster and faster. The ache between my legs starts to get so intense, that's when Kyle rubs my clit once more, and I can't help but scream out his name. When my breathing becomes more even, Kyle sets my legs down.

I'm scared to look up, to see regret or sympathy again like last time. But I feel Kyle's finger touch my bottom lip. When I look up, I see hunger, want. He leans down and kisses me gently. I savor the kiss, never wanting it to end. Kyle presses his body against mine again. This kiss, isn't rough, lusted. It's him showing me, what I wanted from him sooner, comfort, feeling wanted. But it's a little too late. I pull away. I see the confusion in his eyes. He has been with other girls, I can't forget that.

"What's wrong?" Kyle says, trying to walk closer to me, but I put my hands up to stop him.

"I can't do this, I'm sorry." I feel my body telling me no, yelling at him to hold me again. But my head is telling me he chooses now to be what I wanted after he had to be between other girls legs first.

"Do what?"

"Us, it's too late."

"No, I am sorry how I handled things before, but I need you, I miss you." Kyle pleads with me. I can't help but the tear that's slides down my cheek. Why couldn't he fought for me when I was ending things? Why now?

"You miss having the little puppy follow you, looking up at you like you're some kind of God. You bored now with the girls at school? Is that it? Last night you looked fine with that girl." I start to feel the anger again. I hate how easily I get angry, but Kyle and my parents bring the worse out in me.

"I told you, I tried to move on from you, but the other girls meant nothing to me. I wanted you. I haven't slept with anyone. I thought I could last night, but I couldn't."

"Because I saw you."

"No, seeing you made me realize that I was being stupid, trying to forget you when all I wanted is to be with you. I should've fought for us, but I was scared. I was blaming myself for what happened. Hearing you blame me, I felt my heart-shattering, you confirming it. I thought I was doing the right thing, by doing what you wanted."

"Alison everything ok?" Derek says walking toward us. I didn't even hear his car pull up.

"Yeah, sorry."

"You sure?" Derek says standing at my side. I look at Kyle, who is glaring at Derek. I feel like nothing has changed. He's looking at him with pure hatred, but we have done nothing wrong. It's Kyle who has messed up.

"Yeah let's go," I say, walking towards Derek's car.

"Als, please. You can't walk away like this." Kyle grabs my arm and looks into my eyes. I feel my body respond to him, but I shake it off and step back, away from his grasp.

"I can't right now, I'm sorry." I walk away, not looking back. When I sit in Derek's car. I keep my eyes on my lap, till I know I'm away from my house, away from Kyle.

"You ok?" Derek asks looking at me quickly before facing the road again.

"No, not really. My head is all over the place, and Kyle just decided to make it worse. Where was he when I needed him? He's been back to his old ways fooling with other girls, and now he wants me back. I can't handle this right now. We ended things for a reason. He wasn't there for me. He was pushing me away." Oh God I'm just spilling my guts all over Derek, he doesn't need to hear this. "I'm sorry Derek, I'm putting a downer on our night, just ignore me."

"Don't be stupid, I'm here if you ever need to offload. I told you that before. With Kyle, I don't know what to say about that, but follow how you feel. Don't feel you have to do things to make others happy. You said you ended things for a good reason, you stick by them. You have so much going on right now, so maybe you should just stay friends with Kyle, if you want him back in your life, wait till your hundred percent on what you want. Enjoy your life a little, don't let all this weight bring you down."

"Wow, you're wise aren't you?" I giggle and Derek chuckles at me.

"I have my moments." Derek holds my hand, and I let him, I need his comfort right now.

"You have plenty of moments," I say and look out the window.

"By the way, I forgot to tell you because of the whole Kyle thing, but you look amazing tonight," Derek says giving me a big smile, and I can't help but smile back at him. Something about Derek that I'm starting to feel comfortable around again.

"Thank you, you look good too," he does. He's wearing a black shirt, the sleeves rolled up his arms. The shirt fits tightly against his body, giving you an idea of what his body looks like underneath. He's wearing black jeans to match. He almost looks like a bad boy. I realized, his fashion sense is similar to Kyle's. Am I attracted to Derek because of the similarities? No, their personalities are completely different. I remember Derek showing his possessive side, then I remember Kyle showing his on my first day back at school before Derek showed up. Are Kyle and Derek so similar, that I haven't even noticed? I push it away. I wouldn't hang out with someone just because they remind of someone else.

Derek talks about anything and everything, making me forget about the whole Kyle ordeal. Derek is a funny guy, I can't help but laugh at some of his stories, I think it's because most them involves Tom doing stupid stunts. When we get to the party, my side hurts from all the laughing I have been doing. I feel lighter and ready to enjoy myself.

This party has a swimming pool in the front, and so many girls are in their underwear already, splashing around as most guys drink from their cups, watching. Derek takes my hand and guides me inside. He must have been here before, as he knows where we are going. He takes me down some stairs that lead us to a room, where there's a proper bar and dancing area. If I didn't walk inside the house myself, I would swear this looks like a pub. Derek orders some beers and two shots. I raise my eyebrow at him. Shots again, after this morning, I don't know if I could handle all that again.

"This will make you feel better, but if you want just the beer, that's fine. No, pressure." Derek says in my ear, as the music is getting a little loud.

"Nah, I want to let loose a little, tired of being the goody goody all the time," I raise my shot and down it. I can't help but cough after. God I forgot how strong these were.

"Woo," Derek picks up his shot and does his, unlike me, he didn't cough after.

"You want to dance?"

"Really, you want to dance?" I can't help but smile, most guys hate to dance.

"Really, come on" He takes my hand once again and pulls me on the dancefloor, that's crowded with a few couples. The song is Justin Timberlake, "sexy back". I can't help but move my hips to the music. I watch Derek dance, and can't help but laugh at his moves. He definitely doesn't have rhythm, but he doesn't care. He smiles at me, and I smile back. Derek kisses my cheek, I'm sure I blush, but Derek just continues dancing so I do the same.

thirteen

Derek and I, continue to drink beers and take shots. My body is so fuzzy I feel like I'm dancing on a cloud. I start to feel really hot, so I ask Derek, well slur to Derek that I want some fresh air. I crawl up the stairs and stumble to the front of the house. I go the end of the pool away from the crowd and sit down. I take my boots off and dangle my feet in the water. It feels so refreshing, I just lean on my hands and look up into the sky.

"You having fun?" Derek sits down next to me. I forgot he was behind me. Drinking does screw with your mind.

"Yeah, my body feels so light. My mind is so clear. No wonder why people drink all the time. It takes away the bad."

"Yeah, but only for a small amount of time, but drinking makes you do stupid things. Look at me. I had a few drinks because my parents were on my case, I did something stupid with Savannah. I feel like it wasn't me. So don't drink your problems away all the time, it takes you down on a dark path."

"I think we are being too serious right now. No more serious talk, just nice talk," I say and giggle.

"Nice talk, I can do that." Derek takes his shoes and socks off and dangles his feet in the water too.

"Look who it is, the virgin Mary." I look across from me to see Trina, smirking at me. Oh no, I'm in no state to deal with her right now.

"Back off Trina," Derek says angrily to her.

"Why what you going to do? Screw me in the laundry room, behind Alison's back? All you have to do is ask." Trina laughs at me.

"Wouldn't touch you, even if you paid me. Not that desperate."

"You must be if you are crawling back to this cocktease. You do know why Kyle ended it with her? She is harder to get into than the playboy mansion." I broke it up with Kyle, not the other way round.

"Get your facts right, bitch. I ended it with Kyle, not the other way round. Just because you started spreading your legs open, doesn't mean every girl should. Some people have more respect." I seethe and stand up. I grab a towel that is lying on one of the lounge chairs and dry my feet before putting my boots back on. I think I'm sobering up now.

"Come say that to my face, you should be careful, wouldn't want something bad to happen to you again. Always watch your back. That's the saying isn't it?" Trina has such an evil grin on her face, I want to slap it right off. I walk up to her, I see the shock on her face for a split second, and then it's gone. Replaced by her signature smirk. "What you going to do goody- goody? Call me some names?" Trina laughs at my face.

The anger I always seem to carry, builds up. I am not letting this skank bully me. I dealt with Savannah for years, I'm not letting Trina think she can do the same, that I will just stand there and take it. I pull my fist back and punch her in the face. Trina is in such shock, she stumbles back and lands on the ground, groaning in pain. I sit on top of her and punch her again.

"Didn't Savannah tell you, I punched her in school, then again at a party? I'm not letting a piece of cheap trash like you bully me. You are a piece of shit on my shoe, nothing more. You are pathetic," I punch her again. I feel arms wrap around me and pull me away. I look down at Trina and she's crying, staring at me. I smile, I mean I smile with pure hatred, I see her flinch away. It felt so good hitting her, spewing all the hate and anger I have on her, I didn't want to stop

"You talk shit about me again, I will hurt you, that's a fucking promise." Trina looks at her friends, but they look anywhere but at her. She stands up and I see her lip is split and covered in blood, and her eye is starting to swell shut. She looks at me once again. All her smugness is gone. She leaves the party.

I look around the party and once again, people gathered around to see the fight. I bet they aren't surprised anymore that it's me that's involved again. I hear cheers and whistles. I can't believe that just happened. Some people gather around me and Derek, telling me what badass I am. I laugh with few people, who I haven't spoken to before.

"Wow, didn't think you had it in you. Glad you stuck up for yourself," Derek says.

"She went too far, and I'm not letting someone else start to bully me."

"Savannah still giving you a rough time?" Derek flinches realizing that he has brought her up.

"No, she is actually nice to me now, she even stuck up for me when Trina first laying it on me." I can see the shock in Derek's eyes. Yeah, guess it's still shocking hearing Savannah be like that.

"Wow, people can change. I'm glad she's backed off. Hopefully, Trina has now too. She would be an idiot if she did anything again."

"You guys want a shot?" A guy with strawberry blond hair asks, holding a tray of shots like Tom did at his party. I grab two and down one after the other. Derek does the same.

"Right on girl," the guy says, then walks on to other people.

"Think I'm turning into a bad influence on you," Derek chuckles, he guides me back downstairs to the dancefloor. They started playing cheesy music. I can't help but laugh and sing along to the words. The shots have started kicking in again, making me have that happy buzz.

I'm in the middle of the dance floor, grinding my bum against Derek's front, and I don't care. I feel like I don't have a care in the world. I had a few more shots and danced some more to the point I'm having the time of my life. There's a girl, dancing in front of me, her hand on my hip and she's moving with me. We are both smiling and singing towards the song. I never want this night to ever end. A new song comes on, and Derek spins me around, so I'm facing him, he has the same smile as I probably have on my face. The next thing I know, his lips are on mine.

I am in shock for a second, my head feels so cloudy, and then I start to kiss him back. It's nice and gentle. His lips are soft against mine. He licks my bottom lip and I open my mouth for him, I touch his tongue with mine. He pulls me closer to him, and I wrap my arms around his neck. A voice in my head is telling me to stop, this isn't right, but I can hardly hear it. When Derek steps back, I can see the hunger in his eyes, the same look Kyle used to give me. But even though I know I'm a little drunk, I won't go any further than this. I'm not ready for that. As Derek can sense it, he smiles, and gives me a quick peck on the lips and starts dancing with me again. Making sure the kiss doesn't leave us uncomfortable.

I wake up with my head banging, so much worse than what it was yesterday morning. God, where am I? I look around and see I'm in a room I've never seen before. The walls are light blue, I see a desk full of papers, with a bookshelf on top. I sit up resting my head against the headboard, and I feel like I'm dying. I look around for any sign to where I am when I see pictures of Derek on the walls, I guess I'm at his house.

I start to panic on why I'm here, as my head is a little fuzzy on what happened at the end of the party. I look down at my clothes and see I'm still fully dressed, thank God for that. I see a glass of water and some Tylenol. I take the tablets and drink all the water. I sit there and start to remember bits and pieces and groan into my hands. I remember punching Trina and kissing Derek, God Lex is going to kill me.

I don't even want to think what my parents are going to say, I stayed out all night, and I haven't let them know that I'm safe. I'm never going to hear the end of this. I stand up and my head feels so heavy. I groan as I make it to the door and open it slightly to see if I can hear anyone. When I don't, I walk down the hallway and try and find the bathroom, after few doors that lead to bedrooms, I finally find the bathroom, I look in the mirror and I look like a corpse. Bloody hell. I run the cold water and wash my face, I look pale, but least I look a little bit better. I grab some toothpaste and put it on my finger and do a little clean up on my teeth. My mouth is so dry, I feel like I swallowed sand in my sleep. When I feel better, I decide it's time to walk downstairs and find a way to head home.

I hear music playing, so I follow the sound and it leads me to a kitchen, Derek is at the stove cooking. Why does he look so fresh, and I feel I've been run over by a truck. I sit at the breakfast island and wait for Derek to notice me. He starts to dance and wiggle his butt, and I can't help but laugh, causing him to turn around.

"God woman, you scared the crap out of me. How you feeling?" Derek asks as he walks to the fridge and pours me some orange juice. I greedily drink it all, and Derek fills my glass back up, before putting it away.

"Feel worse than what I did yesterday morning. Why do you look like you didn't drink a drop last night? You drank the same amount as me." I sip slowly on my orange juice, it glides down nicely.

"I'm used to it, this is still new to you. Your body isn't use to it yet." Derek plates up some bacon and eggs and he sits opposite me and starts to dig in. My mouth waters, and I happily start to eat up. "Good?" I nod my head, mouth full of eggs,

"Thank you for breakfast, but why am I here?"

"You must have been really drunk. You could hardly stand, you kept saying you didn't want to go back to your prison of a home and started getting all panicky, so I got a cab and took us back here. Don't worry I slept on the couch, when your head hit that pillow, you were out like a light."

"Oh God, I'm sorry. Keep apologizing to you these days. Thank you for looking after me." I rub my fingers against my temples. I still don't want to go home, but better face the music now.

"You ok?"

"No, my parents are going to kill me," I groan into my hands.

"I hope you didn't mind, but I texted them saying you were shopping with a girlfriend, don't think they would appreciate you staying here, but I knew they would worry. I didn't want the police knocking down my door." Thank God for that, least they knew I'm safe.

"Thank you, Derek, you're a Godsend, least they won't be as harsh with me."

"I know parents worry if you don't go back home. Let me clean up here and I will drive you back," Derek stands up and starts to clear away the dishes.

"Isn't your car at the party?"

"Going to use the spare car, it's in case of emergencies, I will collect my car later."

"Thanks, Derek, I really mean that."

"Anytime Alison."

fourteen

I barely got to the door, when the door flew open, making me stumble forward. I look up to see my parents looking down at me. I never felt so small in my life. My mom's eyes look all puffy so she must have been crying for hours, and my dad is looking at me with so much disappointment.

"Where the hell have you been?" Dad yells at me. I don't think my dad has ever yelled at me.

"Gerald," Mom puts her hand on his arm, but he doesn't pay attention to her, his eyes are solely on me.

"Well?"

"I went to a party and crashed with a friend. Didn't want to wake you guys up, when I came in."

"Oh wow, thanks for the consideration, even though we knew you didn't stop at a girlfriends. We called Lex and she had no clue where you were going. When we asked about any of your friends who are girls, Lex stammered to long, for us to know, you don't have any female friends."

"Gerald." Mom pleads with Dad, I feel like I want to cry. In two days, he's just admitted that I don't have friends. How pathetic is that, that my dad has to point out how friendless I am.

"No, I'm sick of walking on eggshells in my own house. She needs to show more respect to us." Dad points his finger at me. I feel I want to burst into tears and run to my room. In my head, all I think of is how they both have been nagging at me, I've been avoiding them, so how am I making them walk on egg shells? I went to two parties, two and apparently I'm now a trouble maker. I feel the anger, I hold onto it.

"I never asked you to walk on eggshells around me. I want you to act normal around me. It's you, who keeps thinking I'm going to have a break down any second. All this is in your head. I have always done what I have been told, been the good little girl, and look where that got me. I got bullied and tortured for years. No one knew I existed, even though my two best friends are basically popular, yet I was still invisible. When I do try and get myself out there, I get stabbed, twice. I am living for today and what? I'm getting told off for it. This is BULLSHIT!" I yell and walk past my parents and run to my room and lock the door. I grab out my suitcase and start to pack few clothes, I can't stay here another second. They either smother me or treat me like crap when I try and experience being a normal teenage girl.

"Alison Marie McCartney, you open this door right now." Dad bangs on my door, but I ignore him. I can't get to the bathroom and get my toiletries, I will just have to buy new stuff. When I look around my room, I feel nothing. This was never my room. Caitlin ruined that for me. I take a deep breath and open the door, and see Mom and Dad standing there.

"Where the hell do you think you're going?" Dad says grabbing my arm, and I pull my arm out of his grasp. What is it with men grabbing me?

"Don't you dare touch me? I'm leaving. You don't have to worry about walking on eggshells around your troublesome daughter." I walk downstairs.

"Gerald, do something. I'm not losing my baby," Mom begs and cried, chasing me down the stairs. "Alison, please. We are just worried about you."

"I told you before, how am I meant to move on if you don't let what happened go? I'm not the one who is stuck on what happened. I'm not living in a house where I get told off for acting like a normal girl. Kids go to parties and get drunk. Bet, you guys, did the same thing at my age. I need to breath, and I can no longer do that here.

"We will do better," Mom begs, but I keep walking.

"She's bluffing, let her go, she will be back," Dad says from the top of the stairs. I look at him, and he isn't the loving father I looked up to. I see a very angry man, staring at me. I feel the tears start to build up.

"Gerald." Mom yells at Dad, but I open the front door and walk outside. I take deep breath and decide I will make a decision where to go after I made some distance. Mom runs up to me and hugs me from behind.

"Please don't leave me, your father is just upset. He doesn't mean it." I turn and hug my mom, she returns tightly.

"I'm sorry Mom, need to do this, will text you when I get settled. Love you." I take a few steps back.

"Love you too," I watch the tears fall down my mom's cheek, I feel an ache in my chest, but I ignore it and walk away. Walking away from my childhood home, walking away from my parents.

I keep walking till I reach the park I sometimes run to. I sit on the bench and I feel my whole world is crumbling around me. I don't know why I left. I don't know what I'm doing anymore. All this isn't me, I don't know who I am, what I'm doing. I'm letting anger control my body and actions. Those actions lost me a best friend, my home, and parents. I look out and see families smiling and laughing, and I can't help but start to cry.

Dad over exaggerated, but so have I. I've only been thinking about me, and not caring about anyone else's feelings. I think of last night with Kyle, he was pleading with me, and I was too hurt and angry at him to really listen to what he was saying. He was trying to move on, he was going through some stuff as well, and I didn't want to listen to it. I wanted him to comfort me and need me, I never asked what he wanted, what he was going through.

I shouldn't blame him for the whole Caitlin thing. He didn't know what would've happened. I have helped push him away. I was never alone with him, was scared what we were feeling. I think I was scared to know what was going on in his head. I did the cowardly thing and ended things without giving him a chance. It's not like I was telling him what I was feeling, what I am going through. He isn't a mind reader, but neither am I. We both made mistakes, we were too proud to open up to the other. When Kyle tried, I walked away. Walked away to Derek.

God Derek, after last night, I'm sure I lead him on. I kissed him. I groan out Loud and feel, I'm making one mistake after the other. Lex knew I went to a party and never told her. She's going to find out about me fighting with Trina and making out with Derek. I can just picture her rolling her eyes at me and giving me a good talking to, telling me what an idiot I am. Wow, looking forward to that.

I don't know how long I sit here, but it starts to get dark. I need to decide on where to go. I'm not ready to go back home yet. I will, I know I need to make peace, try and get my life on the right path again but feel we could use this little break. I can't go to Lex's as not ready to face her. Yes I'm a chicken, and to be honest I'm a little scared of her. I know I'm going to get a good telling off from her. I have a thought in my head and hope I'm not going crazy as I start to walk.

I walk away from the park, and head to the rich side of town. I look at all the houses and feel I would need to win the lottery if I ever want to live here. The streets are so clean and well lit. I see the house, I'm hoping I can stay for a few days, and walk up the pathway. I look at the door and shake my head, maybe I am going crazy. But I don't have anywhere else to go. I knock on the door and wait. I start to hear movement, the door opens to a small woman who looks about 5 ft. Her hair is gray and she gives me a warm smile.

"Hi, can I help you?" The lady asks me.

"Yes, can you tell Savannah, Alison McCartney is here, please."

"Of course, hold on." The lady leaves the door open and walks away. I see a camera, in the door frame, so I bet they have security inside, in case anyone tries to break in. After few minutes, Savannah is at the door and looks at me with confusion. I bet she wasn't expecting me at her door, especially this time of night. She looks at my suitcase, and back at me. Her expression changes to sadness and sympathy for me. I don't know why, but I burst out in tears. Everything that has built up, just flows out of me. Savannah runs to me and holds me. I don't remember walking inside, but Savannah guides me to the living room, and she holds me and rocks me, trying to soothe me.

When I finally start to calm down. I spill what has happened the last couple of days. The first party I went to, Derek, Kyle, Trina, which Savannah smiled at when I told her I punched her, not just once. Tell her about my parents, to me walking away. I explained I sat in the park since, till it started to get dark.

"Why did you decide to come here though? I don't mind you being here, but shocked that you chose here." Savannah says.

"I'm shocked myself, but knew you wouldn't judge me. I think I felt I wanted to be here, it's hard to explain. I'm sorry for putting this on you. Not long ago you hated me, now I'm asking to stay here for a few days.

"I feel flattered, you wanted to come here. No one has ever really asked for my help, well something that doesn't involve money. You stay here as long as you like. I like that we are starting to be friends. Never really had a proper friend before, feels nice." I smile at her, she smiles back.

"Well think we should have a girly sleepover then. Ice-cream, some chick flick, and popcorn. What you say?"

"Only if you let me do your hair, and you do my nails. Seen it in movies and I'm dying to do something with your hair, so jealous of it."

"I'm jealous of your body, will give you my hair, if I can have your body."

"Deal," we both start to laugh. I text Mom saying, I'm safe and that I will ring her tomorrow. The rest of the night, Savannah and I, have a little makeover, have facials and eat till we feel too fat, we can't eat anymore. That night, I fall into a deep sleep.

fifteen

Savannah wakes me Monday morning, and I groan into my pillow, I feel like I'm sleeping on a cloud and I don't want to get off it. I have to go to school and deal with Kyle, Lex, and the gossip mill. This puts me off even more and I hide under the blanket, but Savannah has other plans. She takes the blanket away from me and grabs the pillow my head was laying on, and hits me with it. I look at her in shock and see the smile on her face, not trying to laugh at me. I hit her with the spare pillow, for about five minutes we have a childish pillow fight. Definitely awake now.

"Go shower, and will tell the cook to make us some breakfast," Savannah says as she starts to put on her skirt then boots. God I swear, she looks amazing, and she makes it look easy, so not fair.

"You have a cook?" She's rich of course she's going to have a cook.

"Yeah, my parents like to know I eat properly and healthy."

"Where are your parents? They don't mind me staying do they? Don't want to get you into any trouble." Savannah looks at the ground, I know I already said something wrong.

"They are out of town for a few months, so it's ok you staying here. Don't worry about it." I get off the bed and walk to Savannah and give her a hug.

"Thank you for helping me, being there for me. I know we have a rocky past, but glad we have moved past it."

"Thank you for not hating me, some of the stuff I did, even said was pure nasty. I never really treated anyone else like that. You are a lovely, kind person, I couldn't stop myself. I hate how I was with you. I have to act mean and tough so no one tries to take my title but never wanted to take things that far." She says looking at her fingers.

"Why do you want to be queen bee if the people don't treat you right? You could be happier, just being like us normal folk," we both laugh.

"I like being looked up to. I think my mom expects me to be head girl at school. It's who I am."

"I understand." I don't but don't know what else to say.

"You shower, I'll come back in twenty minutes to take you to the dining room.

"No, problem." I go shower and get ready. But once I'm in the shower, I decided I never want to leave. This place is heaven.

Savannah has a personal driver who takes us to school. Took a while to get the shock look off my face. Savannah and I have been talking since breakfast what I'm going to do about Kyle. I still have no clue. I love him, I always will, but I need to get rid of this anger, it's never going to work if I keep holding this grudge against him. My body still responds to him, but I need more than lust. I need him to be there for me, no matter what. I need him to be strong for us.

When I get to school, I see everyone's eyes bugging out seeing me step out of Savannahs car. To them I bet they think hell has finally frozen over. I feel like it's my first day back again. Least I only have this week, then off for Christmas. I still need to go shopping with Lex, if she isn't ignoring me. Savannah parts ways saying she needs to boss some people about, I need to face the music and speak to Lex.

I get to her locker and decide to wait. Each passing minute, I feel my hands sweating. I would hate if I lost my best friend over a stupid party. This weekend was full of too many mistakes. I'm regretting so many things. I should've waited till after the Christmas holidays before I returned back to school, maybe some of this would have been avoided. Two weeks of school, I could have waited, just like my parents advised, but I am too stubborn. Another regret.

"Now you want to talk to me?" Lex says from behind me, causing me to jump.

"You scared the hell out of me," I say, Lex ignores me and starts putting her books into her locker. "Lex I want to say I'm sorry about not telling you about the party on Saturday. I thought I could handle it, but obviously I couldn't."

"Yeah, no shit. I had to hear all this from someone else, you attacking Trina, drinking to the point of you passing out, don't get me started on you and Derek. I feel like you are slipping away, and I don't know what to do anymore." Lex sighs and leans her back against the lockers.

"I know, I regret Saturday. I wish I never went. Trina mentioned about my stabbing again, and the alcohol didn't help, but I lost it. I couldn't handle her talking to me like that. Derek, stupid mistake. I like him, he's been there for me this last week, but I don't want to be in a relationship with him."

"Well, guess you probably have scolded yourself. What is the deal with your parents? They rang me asking about the party, they tried ringing me last night, asking if I saw you. Where were you? Please don't say with Derek."

"My parents and I had a huge fight, I mean the hugest. Dad and I went at it, and I packed my stuff and left." Lex looks at me with utter shock that I can't help but shrug at her.

"Why didn't you ring me? Where did you stay? Again, please don't say, Derek." I can't help but roll my eyes.

"I knew you would be angry with me, after the whole thing with the party, I wanted to go where I wasn't frowned upon."

"Don't be silly, yeah I would have my rant, but then I would have comforted you. I'm your best friend, even if you screw up, I'm always going to be your best friend." Lex says giving me a hug.

"I know, I am sorry."

"Well, you didn't answer my question, where did you go?" I brace myself and say the name that's going to cause Lex's eyes to fall out.

"Savannah." Lex starts laughing, ok that wasn't the response I was expecting.

"No, really, where did you go?"

"Savannah."

"You got to be fucking kidding me. Savannah? Savannah, Savannah?" Lex goes on and on till we get to homeroom, about me going to my ex-enemy house. Yup, what a good start of the day.

"I really wish you came to me, I keep feeling that you're trying to push me away at times. Yes, you're going to do things I'm not going to like, but I do things you don't like. Just don't feel like you have to keep things from me. I want to be the person you run to, not hide from," Lex says looking at the table. I feel likes she's trying not to get upset, God when did I start being such a shitty friend.

"Lex, your right. I'm so sorry. I was so worried you were going to hate me and get all angry, I just knew I didn't want to face it. I don't know why I went to Savannah of all people, but I just went where my gut told me. I really am sorry. Forgive me?" I look into her eyes, I know she has already forgiven me, but I can tell she stills feel hurt. That I went to the one person who treated me like shit, and not my best friend.

"You know you're forgiven, but don't push me away ok? You're my best friend, you're my sister." I stand up and hug Lex, and some guys in class start whistling and whooping. God guys at this school are so immature.

"Just glad you didn't go to Derek's."

"Yeah, I know."

The rest of class went by, Lex kept glaring at Savannah every chance she got, and I had to poke her with my pen to tell her to stop it. It's going to take a while for Lex to get over this. I look at my list I made when I felt I was falling behind in my classes, I've been marking them off when I feel I've caught up. When I see everything is crossed out, I feel relieved that I'm no longer behind. I'm always the one ahead, glad that I'm back on track. Educational wise, I'm doing great. Home life is crumbling and between Derek and Kyle, I feel like I have no clue what I want.

I know I can't go back there with Derek. Can I? He has been there for me, comforting me when I needed it. He has listened to me complain and whine, more than a guy should. He hasn't pushed me. I know he has learned from his mistakes, but I know if I went back there, I would have trust issues with him, especially if he was drinking, any girl could whisper in his ear.

Kyle, well my body still craves him. I miss being how we use to be, but I'm no longer that naive girl. He didn't take long to start hooking up with other girls. He's saying he hasn't slept with anyone, but he didn't say if he did more than kissing. Just imagining another girls mouths on any part of his body, pisses me off. He's sorry, but where was this, when I was ending things. He didn't fight for our relationship, he accepted it.

I hate how my mind is consumed by these two guys in my life. Least my mind is away from Caitlin. I haven't decided if I'm going to court next Monday. I need to go, for closure. Well, that's what I keep telling myself. But first I need to sort things at home. I can't be this angry girl anymore, especially with them. I need help mentally, as well as emotionally. I must be scared more than what I thought. The nightmares don't help. I can't live my life like this. I can't go back, but I need to move forward. But is there room for a guy right now? If so which one?

sixteen

I'm so hungry, my stomach is rumbling. I'm glad my appetite is coming back, but it's coming back with a vengeance. I feel now that I know I need help, and to sort things out with my parents, my body feels a little relaxed. I was in my own head, I didn't click on when an arm comes out and grabs me into a closet. I'm about to scream when I feel my body tingle and realize straight away it's Kyle. Why is Kyle dragging me into a closet? I look around and realize we are in the supply room. When I look up to see Kyle, I'm wondering what he is up to, he looks angry. Why is angry? Oh God is he angry that I left him standing there when I left with Derek on Saturday?

"Kyle. Listen..." I don't even get a chance to finish my sentence as Kyle stands closer and interrupts me.

"You kissed Derek," it isn't a question, he's stating a fact. I just nod, I don't know what to say to that. "You together now?" I feel the anger flowing off him, I know I can't lie.

"I don't know what we are." It's the truth, my mind has been going over and over if I want to be with anyone romantically, and if I do, do I want to be with Derek? Kyle takes a deep breath, probably trying to calm himself down.

"I don't like it." I look at him, shocked that he just said that. He has been kissing countless other girls I bet, and he doesn't like me kissing someone else. Well whoopie do, that's tough shit.

"Well I don't like you kissing other girls, but guess what, life ain't fair." I feel the anger building inside me again, God I'm starting to get a headache from all this anger. "I kissed one guy, one. I did it as I was drinking, plus I wasn't expecting it. You..." I poke his chest. "You, have been hooking up with God knows how many girls and you have to drag me here like a bloody caveman and say you don't like it. Well, tough shit. I will kiss and mess around with whoever I want. If it's with Derek, it's none of your business." I take a deep breath in.

"I never fucked anyone." Is he kidding me?

"Who cares if you haven't fucked them, I bet you've done other stuff." Kyle looks down at the ground. I get my answer. I feel the anger go, sadness takes over. I need to get away. I can't be with him. I go towards the door, but Kyle pins me against the door, his front to my back. I can feel his breath on my neck. I'm having a bit of Deja vu.

I can't move, my body is frozen, my body is begging for his touch. When I feel his hands move my hair to over my shoulder, I feel his fingers graze my skin, and I suck in a breath. Just a little touch, my skin is already burning. Kyle moves his lips to my shoulder, but he doesn't touch, it just hovers, I just want his lips on me, anywhere. I'm starting to pant, and he's barely touched me. I know Kyle is sensing that I'm not going anywhere.

When his tongue licks up my neck, I feel the ache start to build. I can feel his erection press against my lower back. I can't help but grind my ass against him, causing him to hiss in my ear. He spins me around so fast, I almost stumble over. Kyle pins me again against the door and presses his erection against me, grinding himself against my core. God I can feel how hard he is. I start to push against him, trying to ease the ache, but it's making it worse. I can't help the moan that leaves my mouth. Kyle's lips slam down on me. Devouring me. I kiss him with everything in me.

My hands are in Kyle's hair pulling and tugging. I can't get enough. I need this. My head is telling me to slow things down. But all thoughts, everything has gone. My mind is now turned to mush. Kyle lifts me up, I wrap my legs around him. I feel him press against me again, causing me to scream.

"Kyle. Please don't stop," I can't help but how my words come out quivering. I feel that release building inside me, I need this release, need it more than air.

"Fuck no," Kyle grunts into my neck. He then puts his mouth on me again. Kyle uses one hand and starts to push up my dress a little more, even though it's already around my waist. So glad that I decided on a dress today.

Kyle slides his finger over the fabric that is covering my most personal area. I arch against his hand. I need him to touch me. It feels like forever till he finally rubs against my clit. I know I'm so close. He rubs harder and starts to finger against my wet folds. I can hear the wet sounds, but I don't care. He adds another finger inside me, stretching me. Touching where I need him.

"You're so fucking wet, so fucking tight. I missed this, I missed you." I can't properly process his words, I'm about to orgasm any second. "You belong to me, your body belongs to me. Your body knows it. You own me. God I want you so fucking badly. Fuck." I can't help but scream out Kyle's name when I orgasm so hard that my eyes roll back. When I finally start to calm down, I look into Kyle's eyes, and I see hunger, want, and need. I feel my body respond to him all over again. I just want to say fuck it and tell him to take me, right here, against the wall. Kyle's eyes go darker, knowing what my thoughts have gone too.

Kyle places my underwear back in place and he undoes his jeans and pulls out his hard erection, leaving his boxers still on. I can't believe he's got it out. My breath catches when I see it. He is so smooth that I can't help but lick my lips and Kyle groans. He wraps his hands around it and starts to stroke himself, with me still pressed against the door, but he has released one of my legs, but one leg is still wrapped around his hip. He's that close, I can feel the heat from his erection against my opening, which means he can feel my heat. He strokes himself harder, faster, but his eyes stay on me. This is so fucking hot. I stand there just watching him masturbate, and I just want him inside me.

"You need to stop looking at me like you could eat me, or I won't be able to stop doing something that should be saved for somewhere better," Kyle growls at me. He actually growled at me. I feel myself getting turned on. I read books where men talk dirty, demand women but never knew it could be such a turn on. I feel I want him to touch me again. "Touch yourself for me. I can feel your heat rolling off you near my cock. Let me watch you, touch yourself." Oh my God, has Kyle really asked that? I hesitate for a second, then I reach down into my underwear, feeling weird at this angle as one leg is still around Kyle, but I adjust.

I feel the wetness already, my underwear is soaked. I push my head against the wall, and start to rub myself. Because I feel quite sensitive already, it doesn't take long till I'm coming again. Kyle comes right after. When I look down, I see his come, all over his hand and some hits the floor. I look at his hand, and I wonder what it tastes like. Before Kyle has a chance to clean himself, I grab his hand and lick. It's not as bad as I thought it would be. I lick my lips causing Kyle to groan again. I can't help but smile. Right now, I feel so blissfully happy.

"That was so fucking hot," Kyle kisses me again, but this time it's gentle, I can't help but sigh into him. "I want you to be mine again, only mine." I look up and stand back. All my thoughts coming rushing back. He had to ruin it, didn't he?

"Kyle..."

"No, you want me, just as badly as I want you. I shouldn't have treated you like you were glass. You are one of the strongest people I know, I shouldn't have treated you differently. I need you, I know you need me." I shake my head, trying to process what he is saying.

"Kyle, you can't just take me into a room, again and please me, then throw a curve ball at me. I don't get what you want half the time."

"I want you, it's always been you. I want you back. Please, give me another chance." I look into Kyle's eyes, I swear, they are like my kryptonite.

"I don't know, my head is all over the place. I don't think I'm ready to start anything, not till I sort things out first." I say pleading with him not to put me in this situation.

"What sort of things?"

"My parents mostly, we aren't in a good place right now, I have Caitlin's court hearing on Monday. I need time."

"Time, I can do that. Just don't cross me off yet." Kyle takes my hand and I feel the electricity rush through my entire body.

"I won't." I stand up and kiss his lips softly, but he presses me against the wall and kisses me so passionately that my legs turn to jelly. When he steps back, he has a huge smile on his face.

"Just in case you forgot what our kiss is like."

"Like I could forget," I giggle as I open the door and step out into the hallway, I look both ways, but no one is about.

"Als?" Kyle yells out as I start to walk towards the cafeteria.

"Yeah?"

"If you ever need to talk, I'm here. About anything. I rather be your friend, than not in your life, just know that." I give him a small smile. I rather him be in my life than not at all.

"Thanks, Kyle." I give a little wave and turn. I feel my whole body vibrating. My body is always going to respond to Kyle, but I don't want it to be just lust that keeps us together. Deep down, I know it's more than that, he's my best friend, even though it's been a hard week, coming back, ending things with Kyle, falling out with my parents. I know I will always need him. He's a part of me, I can't change that. But that leaves me to what do I do now.

When I sit down next to Lex, she gives me a knowing smile. Is this woman psychic? But this is Lex, anything with sex, she knows. Even though, I didn't have sex with Kyle, even though I wanted to. How does she know I wasn't with Derek? But Derek is at the table talking to Tom, so the first clue is there. I feel eyes on me and when I look around my eyes land on Kyle at his table, and he is staring at me. I feel my body start to ache for him, I just had two orgasms in the space of twenty minutes. I just want to walk over there and straddle him. I need to snap my head out of it. I hear a chuckle beside me, I know Lex knows it's Kyle as it doesn't take a detective to guess that two of us have done something. Derek and everyone else though is oblivious to what we got up to.

seventeen

L ex took me to Savannah's to get my things. Her parents are on a second honeymoon, and Lex wants me to stay with her till I sort things out with my parents. Savannah was understanding and wasn't surprised when Lex came with me. I think Savannah knew that Lex wouldn't be happy that I chose her over my best friend. When I arrived at Lex's home, I sprawled out on her couch. It's been one of those days that just wipe you out. I close my eyes and start to relax. Should've known it wouldn't last.

"What happened between you and Kyle?" Lex jumps on me, causing me to grunt.

"How do you know we did anything?" I feel my face heating up, so it's already a giveaway. Stupid body reactions.

"One, you and Kyle didn't show up till twenty minutes after the bell rang. Second, you had a fuck me glow that you get after having an orgasm. Thirdly, the way Kyle was looking at you like he could eat you, the way you looked at him like you could fuck him there in front of everyone, such a giveaway. So don't hide this shit from me, spill." I roll my eyes. God can't hide anything from her.

"First, we didn't have sex. Secondly I had two orgasms, and thirdly, he wants us to get back together."

"Wow, two orgasms in twenty minutes, fucking hell. You have to keep him." I can't help but laugh.

"He's not a dog, Lex."

"I know, but damn girl. Seriously though, what did you say? After two orgasms I would have done anything he said, good thing I don't see Kyle like that though." Yeah, a real good thing.

"I told him I'm not ready to start anything with anyone. I told him I need to sort things out with my life, but he told me to keep him in mind. That he will wait till I'm ready to decide. But I don't want him putting his life on hold waiting for me." I can't help give out a loud sigh.

"Least you told him how you felt, if he's willing to wait till you know what you want, then least you know that he will stop being with other girls."

"That's the thing, how do I get past the other girls thing. I hate that he's been with them, especially shortly after our break up."

"Men are weird and handle things badly, especially when they are hurting and confused. I'm not defending him, but he must realize how important you are to fight what he wants. Just get your head on straight, then follow your heart. He will understand, no matter what you choose." Lex says holding my hand.

"I know, he told me he wants to be friends, that he rather have me in his life than not at all."

"See. Don't think about it now. Just wait till you're ready."

"Thanks, Lex."

"Anytime. Seriously though, two orgasms?" I laugh and hit Lex with the pillow.

We have a girly night, especially after I told her about my girly night with Savannah. We watched some comedies and ate till we felt like we were going to explode. We didn't bring up Derek or Kyle, which I appreciated. I even let Lex do my nails, a different color for each finger. James rang Lex, she disappeared for thirty minutes and when she came back, she had a goofy looking smile on her face, and I can tell she had her own orgasm. But unlike her, I didn't want to know the details. When we decided to go to bed, I passed out as soon as my head reached the pillow.

I'm in the bathroom that's connected to the school gym. I look down to see me wearing my Halloween costume. Why am I here? My mind is telling me to leave, but I can't. I don't know why I should leave. I hear movement to my side and I see Caitlin looking in the mirror, staring at me. There's something in her eyes that causes my skin to prickle. I can't figure out why she is looking at me like that. I'm having a sense of Deja vu, but I can't figure out why. My body is telling me to run, but I can't follow its instruction.

"Yeah I am, are you?" Caitlin asks giving me a smile. I shake my head.

"Sorry, what?" I ask.

"You asked me if I'm having a good time, you ok?"

"Yeah sorry, feeling kind of out of it, think I'm going to get back out there." I start to walk to the door.

"You going with Kyle?" I should tell her no, but for some reason I nod.

"Too bad you're leaving, but I understand," Caitlin says looking down.

"Have you heard any news on your date?" I don't know where that question came from, it feels like it came out on auto-pilot. Like that's what I am meant to say.

"He's just waiting, don't you worry, I always get my man," Caitlin says giving me a wink. I have warning bells in my head. I say goodbye and open the door. I see loads of people dancing, but I know I need to run to Kyle. I push my way through the crowd. I keep walking, stepping around everyone. I feel like this is never ending. I sense someone behind me, but I don't turn around. I need to find Kyle.

I finally see him, I start to run towards him. I see his eyes land on me, his smile just warms me up, but I know I need to reach him, I can't stop. But when I feel like I'm only a few steps away, I hear a scream. I turn and I see Caitlin standing there, looking down at someone. I follow her line of sight and see myself on my knees. I see the blood spilling from my back, all over the white dress. I look at Caitlin and she has two big police guys holding her back. She looks angry. I see tears falling down her face.

I watch Kyle fall down on his knees and hold the other me. I feel like I'm having an out of body experience just watching this. I just stand and watch, I can't move.

I hear myself start to talk to Kyle." I finally get you and I hardly did things that couples do, I didn't even get a chance to sleep with you." The words are so soft, like a whisper.

"Trust me, when you're all better we are going to do everything you want. I'm going to make love to you in a hundred different ways, just to warn you," Kyle says, the other me starts to laugh but ends up coughing. I can feel tears fall down my face, watching the agony in Kyle's eyes.

"Please don't let me die."

"Where the fuck is the ambulance?" I see Lex shout. James trying to hold her.

"Stop saying that, you're not dying." Why can't I move, I can't watch this anymore.

"Don't you dare close your eyes, you stay with me, keep looking at me," Kyle yells, shaking the other me. The tears are falling heavily now. I can't stop the tears as I watch the person I love go through this, watching me die.

"Kyle I... I love you. I think I've always loved you."

"I love you. You were always it for me, so you better keep those big beautiful eyes on me." I watch other me close her eyes, and Kyle is shaking her, shouting at her to wake up. I watch, feeling my heart break. Watching Kyle's pain is the worst feeling ever. I forgot that he told me he loved me. We haven't said it since. I turn my head away, not able to watch anymore. I close my eyes and when I open them again Caitlin is standing there in front of me. Tears in her eyes, but I can still see the anger.

"Why Caitlin? Why did you do this?" I beg of her, but she just stares at me.

"He was mine. He was always meant to be mine. I thought he was it for me." I look at her, and I see the pain there. I then feel pain shoot through my back. I look at Caitlin, but there is nothing in her hands. She's just standing there looking at me. "I'm not the only person who is going to hurt you." I feel the pain again shoot up my back. I scream in pain and agony. Screaming for Kyle, screaming for myself.

"ALISON, ALISON!" I feel a slap across my face waking me up from my nightmare. "Als, shit you scared me half to death. You were screaming for ages, you wouldn't wake up. Had to slap you. It was the most terrifying thing to see. Were you having one of your nightmares?" I nod, not able to talk yet. My whole body is shaking and covered in sweat. That's the most scariest and weird dream so far.

"Shit, never knew they were that bad, I thought your parents were over exaggerating when it came to them, no wonder they are how they are. Fuck me sideways." Lex says sitting next to me. I look into her eyes and see fear in them. I must have really scared her.

"I was back at the Halloween dance. I was in the bathroom with Caitlin, it was all replaying itself. Then I watched myself being stabbed, watching you and Kyle at my side. Watched the pain on Kyle's face, seeing the fear coming from you. I couldn't move, I watched me die." I feel the tears fall down, remembering my dream.

"Oh, honey." Lex hugs me tightly, not caring I'm covering her in my sweat.

"That's not the scariest bit," I tell her, I see her eyes widen, knowing there's more.

"In my dream, I closed my eyes and when I open them Caitlin was standing there, right in front of me, looking at me with pain and anger. She told me she wasn't the only one who tried to hurt me or something. Then I feel the pain in my back, she just stood there, her eyes on me. Not moving. I felt the pain through my body, the agony I went through." I start to sob into Lex's chest. She just holds me. Lex holds me till my sobs stop. She stays quiet. I don't think she knows what to say. I can't go back to sleep. I just see Caitlin staring at me. Lex stays up with me and we put on season one of "Vampire Diaries". Lex stays by my side, being there for me.

eighteen

When the sun starts coming up, I see Lex has finally fallen asleep. I don't blame her, she must be really tired from being up all night with me. I go through her drawers knowing she wouldn't mind. I borrowed a pair of shorts and a T-shirt. I had to change out of my clothes last night as they were soaked with my sweat. I didn't bring anything to run in. When I'm dressed I step outside, I can feel the cold air hit me. I wouldn't be surprised if it snowed soon. I stretched my legs out, then started at a slow pace.

After a few minutes, I felt my body start to unwind. I need to speak to someone about these nightmares. I'm starting to get freaked out by them. The one last night shook me to the core. Remembering Kyle's face, though. Is that what happened? My mind is a little hazy when it comes to the exact details. But the pieces I do remember don't add up. Just watching my two best friends, seeing that. I can't imagine being in that situation. I know if anything bad happened to them my heart would shatter. I couldn't lose them, especially like that.

After seeing that, I can understand a little about what Kyle was going through. Why he acted like he did. I can't accept the other women, but why he treated me like I could break at any second. I can understand why my parents acted all protective. Them getting the phone call about their only daughter at death's door. If I had a child, I would never want them to leave. God, I have been a grade A bitch to them. It's all been about me, I didn't give a damn about their feelings, what they went through.

I keep going at my pace, not wanting to overdo myself. I keep going till I stop at my home. I didn't have a plan on where I was going but guess my body wanted to come here. I sit on my swing and just stare at my house. Flashes of my childhood here running through my head. A tear falls down my cheek thinking how Caitlin has ruined that for me. I hate that I hate my house. I know I'm going to college soon, but I always wanted to feel like I could come home whenever I wanted, but being at home I feel like there's a gray cloud over me.

I don't know how long I sit there, but the front door opens, and I see my mom walk towards me with a steaming hot drink, she passes it to me. I hold it and look at the ground. I can't look her in the eyes. I treated her horrible. My mom, my best friend. Mom sits down on the grass and doesn't say anything, probably worried I would walk away. She's still in her pajamas and night coat. I look up a little and notice the lines around her eyes, how puffy they are. She looks like she has aged. I never noticed.

"I'm sorry Mom," I whisper. I start to cry. Mom picks me off the swing and lets me sit between her legs as she holds me. I cry for being an awful daughter. I cry for not letting my parents in, not asking for help, for pushing them away. I just cry for everything. I need my mommy, I always will. Her just holding me, I feel at peace. She rocks me and strokes my hair.

"It's going to be ok. It's going to be ok. Mommy's here, Mommy's here." I hurt her, more ways than one, she is consoling me, giving me unconditional love, even though I don't deserve it.

"I'm so sorry Mom."

"It's ok, doesn't matter," Mom says still holding me, stroking my hair.

"I hurt you, I never wanted to hurt you. I was hurting as well. I hate how something so bad happened to me. I never did anything wrong. I felt like I was being punished." I say through tears. I need her to understand, why I was how I was.

"We can talk about it later. Just know I'm here for you, we will make it better."

"I love you," I whisper.

"I love you, too.

I look up and see my dad standing in the doorway, I see the remorse on his face. I can tell he knows how sorry I am, by seeing it in my eyes, on my face. I know me being like this is causing him more pain. I don't want them to go through any more pain because of me.

Mom brought me inside after I started to calm down from my little breakdown. Dad has sat opposite me, but he would hardly look at me. Have I hurt him that badly? I remember talking to him with no respect, I was so horrible towards him. I was always his little princess, now I bet he sees me anything but. I feel the tears start to prickle behind my eyes and I take in a few deep breaths, don't want to cry again.

Mom made some hot cocoa with some whipped cream, my favorite. I don't deserve this, I don't deserve Mom being so nice to me. I give her a small smile and wrap my hands around the hot cup. I can't look up, and I don't know where to start, but need to say something.

"I'm sorry for what I put you both through for the past six weeks. I know I haven't been the wonderful daughter you have raised, I have treated you both poorly. Especially the last week. I am sorry." I still don't look up, I don't know if I can.

"We know you were going through something. None of us can imagine what you have been going through. We just wanted to protect you and we didn't know how. You are our baby, even though you're going off to college next year, you will always be our baby." I feel Mom touch my hand, I hold on, wanting her comfort once again. I needed to know she still loved me, cared for me.

"I need to apologize," Dad adds in, I look up in shock, he doesn't need to apologize. I see the pain in his eyes.

"Dad, you have nothing to be sorry for. It was me being a brat. Yes, I was going through stuff, still am, but you didn't deserve any of this."

"I do need to apologize. I didn't know what to do anymore, I felt I was losing my little girl when you started being distant and blanking out both of us, I felt lost. When you started drinking away your troubles, I felt responsible. I didn't want you to go down that dark path where drinking is the only solution. How I handled it wasn't one of my best moments. You are my princess, I should've been there for you. Not goad you on by yelling at you. I was just angry, you didn't deserve it no matter what." I feel the tears slide down my cheeks, and Dad stands up and holds me in his arms. When I look at Mom, she is crying, too. I grab hold of her hand and we stay like that for a while.

I finally tell them about my nightmares, especially the one I had last night. I told them it was so bad I couldn't go back to sleep. I told them what happened at the dance, well from what I can remember. Told them about me in the bathroom and then looking for Kyle to me feeling the shooting pains. I explained it started to get fuzzy, but in my dream it felt so real like I was back there. Mom was crying for me. I never told them what happened. I kept saying I never wanted to talk about it, they never pushed.

Don't know how long I talked, but once I started, I kept going. I told them about Derek being in my life, which Dad wasn't happy hearing. I explained how he has been there for me, to Kyle and I breaking up, even our friendship. I explained how part of me blamed him. Neither of them interrupted me, just stayed quiet till I told them everything. Savannah, Trina, me drinking, to Kyle wanting to be back in my life. After I had finished, I felt better.

"Awww, sweetie, you have gone through so much. I remember high school but never had as much going on as you do. It shows one thing though," Mom says.

"What's that?"

"You are a very strong person. You tried to deal with it the only way you can. You tried to get on with your life. You made some wrong decisions, but we learn from our mistakes."

"I don't feel strong. I am so full of anger at what happened. I hated how you all were treating me so differently. I never once thought about what you all were going through. I just felt I couldn't breathe at times. I should've said something sooner, but didn't know how."

"Your mother's right. You were trying to deal, we tried to give you the space you needed, but when you have children of your own, you'll know that it's hard to pull away. Especially when you can see them hurting. The question is, what do you want to do now?" Dad asks. I pause and think. I need help, I know that. Professional help.

"I need to talk to someone. I know I just explained everything to you, but I need to talk to someone professionally, who can help me deal with all this anger. I feel it build up when someone does or says something I don't like. I don't want to live with it anymore. I want to let it all go, but I don't know how."

"We will get some help then." We talk some more, but I start to feel my eyes getting heavy and mom walks me to my room (my new room) and tucks me into bed. I fall into a dreamless, deep sleep.

When I wake up a few hours later, I woke up with a huge urge to pee. I use the bathroom and walk downstairs. Mom and Dad are on the couch in a deep conversation, I clear my throat to let them know I'm here. They stop talking and ask me to sit down with them. I sit in the middle, and Mom starts to stroke my hair.

"You sleep ok? Any nightmares?" Mom asks concerned.

"Yeah, no dreams, thankfully. What's up?"

"Me and your mother have been talking, and we made a big decision." I look between them, and God they aren't splitting up are they? I will never recover if they split up.

"You two separating?" I feel the tears come after I asked.

"God, no sweetie. Nothing like that," Mom says, I feel my heart calm down, didn't realize it was beating so heavily.

"We decided that even though you will be going to college after the summer, we are going to sell this house and move," Dad says. I can't help but look at him in utter shock. This is our home, I grew up here.

"Why?" I whisper.

"I know it will take getting used to the idea, but when you come home to visit, we don't want you dreading it. You explained how this house feels different now. We understand, it feels different to us as well. Think it's for the best we move. We can choose another nice house. We will still be staying in the area, our jobs and friends are here. Thinking maybe the new houses that were recently built. You can do up your room, making it your own. What do you say?" he asks.

"You sure, I'm sorry I am putting you through this," I feel like I'm being a burden, making them change their lives, well their home.

"We all need a change. We think it's for the best." I look at Mom and Dad, I know they want to start fresh too. We talk about putting the house up for sale, soon as we go through all the procedures. Hoping to be moved into the new home before the summer. After an hour of talking about this new change, I wish them goodnight and tell them I'm heading back to bed. I need more sleep, I feel totally drained. New house. Even though I'm excited, I hate that I will no longer live next door to Kyle. I will be moving away, but feel I'm leaving a part of myself behind.

I text Lex telling her that I talked to my parents and got things sorted, I will talk more tomorrow at school.

Lex: Glad you're all ok, next time text me if you're going to do a disappearing act. Took you all day to reply back. Was going to call the cops.

Me: Sorry, fell asleep, going back to sleep now, see you tomorrow x x

Lex: Night hun, Love you x x

nineteen

"Tell me everything," Lex says when she picks me up the next morning. I roll my eyes at her. No good morning, just straight to the point. I tell her about me going for a run, leading to my parents house, to what we talked about. "Wow, a new house." Yeah wow.

"I know. I know I wanted to move on and that house gives me the heebie geebies, but I feel like I'm leaving my childhood behind me. I'm so screwed up in the head." I say as I put my face in my hands.

"Awww, Hun, yeah you are a little." She chuckles at me, and I hit her arm.

"Thanks," I grumble.

"Anytime," Lex winks at me.

"When do you start seeing the therapist?" Yeah, Mom and Dad said at breakfast they were going to make some calls and get the help I need.

"Parents are looking into it, so will know soon."

"Can't believe you're going to see a therapist. Wonder if you have to lie on the couch as you see on TV."

"Lex, you know how to make me smile." I look at her and laugh.

Leave it to Lex to think something like that.

"Glad I'm good for something. Let me know though, how it goes."

"I will." We talk about going to the mall after school to get some Christmas gifts. I start to plan a list in my head on what to get people. Two people stand out if I should get them something or not.

When I get to school, I step out of the car and I feel like I'm in a movie. On one side is Kyle with his friends, the other is Derek with his. Like they both can sense me, they turn and smile at me, not realizing the other is looking as well. I feel my stomach go in knots. Why do I feel like I have to choose?

"Wow this is awkward," Lex says walking to my side. Yeah, it is.

"Just a little. Come on. Let's just go straight to your locker." We link arms and head inside. I walk past both of them but give them each a smile. God I'm screwed.

Lex keeps quiet, but it doesn't last long when we get to homeroom, and I knew she was biding her time.

"Soooooo..." Lex drawls out. "What you going to do?" God can't I have a normal morning at school? I remember the simpler times. I hated that I thought my life was boring, now I took that life for granted.

"I told you, I'm not ready to see anyone."

"I know that, but you're hanging with Derek. Kyle is looking at you like he could fuck you right there in front of everyone. Neither one is going to like that other guy will be in your life too. Wow did that even make sense?"

"I get what you're saying. I'm not going to keep anything back from either of them. They have to learn to deal with the fact that they are both in my life. If they want to stay in it, they have to deal."

"So, you're going to tell them that?" I know I have to. Not going to hide anything. I'm not doing anything wrong.

"Yeah." I shrug, trying to act that it's no big deal.

"That will be interesting to watch." I roll my eyes at her. Glad my life is entertaining her.

I'm sitting in my seat next to Derek and he is telling Tom about a new comic book hero turning into a movie or something. I'm sitting there spacing out. I don't know why I'm getting so nervous, it's not like Derek is my boyfriend. If he doesn't like that Kyle is going to be back in my life, it's just tough. I take a deep breath and when I'm about to open my mouth, I feel eyes on me, I feel my body start to heat up. Why does my body sense him before I see him? It's so not fair. I look towards Kyle's table and I see him looking at me. I give him a smile, but he just keeps staring at me. God what that one look does to me. I need a distraction.

"Kyle and I are friends again," I say close to yelling. Ok, that wasn't as subtle as I wanted it to be.

"What?" Derek looks at me in confusion. I look around the table, and they all have stopped talking and are watching me. That's all I need.

"Ummm, Kyle and I had a talk, and well, he's apologized to me and wants to be friends again," I say stumbling over my words.

"You said yes?" I don't look up at him, as don't want to see how he's taking this.

"Well kinda, he was a big part of my life, and everyone deserves a second chance, right?" I finally look up, and I swear I see anger, then it's replaced so quickly. But that one look sent shivers all over and not in a good way.

"I understand that, you gave me a second chance. You're a kind person Alison. Just hope he doesn't hurt you." Derek holds my hand, and I'm glad there was no scene or drama.

"Thanks, Derek, I know it will be hard for both of you, but I don't want to lose either of you." I don't. Derek has been my rock for the last couple of weeks. Kyle is well, Kyle. He will always be there.

"You won't. Thanks for telling me." I smile, and I hear groans, some of the guys at the table are disappointed by our interaction. Well, I'm glad that we talked about this maturely.

I eat my lunch and tell Lex and Derek I'm going the bathroom.

Lex asked if she should come, but I rolled my eyes at her. I told her girls don't always need to go to the bathroom together. I leave the cafeteria, and head towards the closest girls toilets. When I get to the door, I feel someone push me in. Why do I keep getting pushed into rooms? I turn and see Kyle, he's so close. I feel the heat coming from him.

"You need to stop dragging me into rooms. I'm `starting to think you have a kink for school rooms," I joke, but Kyle is just staring at me. I look into his eyes and feel I'm being pulled in.

"I need to touch you Als," Kyle says huskily. The words go straight between my legs.

"Kyle..." I whisper.

"I need to feel you." He presses himself against me, I gasp when I feel his hard erection.

"Kyle..."

"Need to taste you." I feel his tongue slightly touch my lips, God I'm aching so badly.

"Kyle..." I'm pretty sure that time it sounded like I was begging. Right now, I would beg. I need him to touch me everywhere.

"I need to know how wet you are for me. I use to hold back when it came to you. Now, almost losing you, I realize I need to give you all of me. All of me wants to taste you right now between your legs. I want you to grind against my face like you did with your hand. Fuck Als, when you were stroking me and getting yourself off with the same hand. I wanted to fuck you so hard. When I first touched between your legs, God I was in heaven." I feel him nip my neck and lick the spot.

He starts to grind himself against me, causing me to moan. His leg is in between mine, I start to grind against him. I need to ease this ache. I can feel how wet I am. He's barely touched me, just his words are sending me over the edge.

"I'm going to be between your legs one day. I will be your first. That belongs to me. Me. I can imagine how tight you will be. How hot. Fuck, I'm getting so hard just thinking about it." God Kyle has never talked like this to me. He always treated me like I was fragile. Now, he is showing me how much he wants me, craves me. I love every second. Didn't think I would like someone talking dirty to me, but with Kyle it's fucking unbelievable.

Kyle picks me up and sits me on the counter near the sinks. He grinds himself against me again. My legs are wrapped so tightly around him, I want to be as close as I can be. I want to please him, he pleased me last time. I need to do this. I need to touch him. His lips are on mine, devouring me. I undo his belt and unzip his jeans. I use my feet to pull them and his boxers down a bit. When I see his smooth, hard erection, I can't help but lick my lips. I wonder what he would taste like in my mouth.

"Fuck, Als." I look up to see him looking at my mouth. I can't help but smile. I wrap my hand around him and start to stroke him up and down. Taking my time. I feel Kyle breathing against my neck. Groaning next to my ear.

I start to pick up speed. Kyle looks down watching me get him off. His forehead is pressed against mine. I feel so turned on, just watching him lose control. I get an idea in my head and I take my hand away. I feel Kyle groan in protest. I look him in the eye, I take my hand and lick it slowly, then wrap it around him again. I feel him go harder. After few minutes, Kyle growls and comes all over my hand breathing fast.

He looks at me with pure adoration. I kiss his lips softly. But the kiss turns into something hot and Kyle quickly gets me off before the bell rings telling us to head to our next class. When I leave the bathroom, Kyle quickly kisses my lips and we part ways. We didn't talk, but there wasn't anything to say. It was perfect, we didn't want to spoil it. I know bringing up Derek, especially after what we did would definitely have spoiled it.

twenty

My head has been in a daze since I parted away from Kyle. I told him I wasn't ready for a relationship, yet he can't keep his hands to himself. I think how his hands felt on me. I feel my body react, I need to stop thinking about him. I do not want to start getting turned on during gym class. I need to talk to him. Part of me hates what I have to say, but how am I meant to sort out my head if my brain turns to mush when he touches me. I need to keep a straight head. I need to get my home life back on track and get the Caitlin court thing over with. We said friends and friends don't do that. I think back on how our friendship was like, we did start to blur the lines towards the end. Were we always like this? Now there's no holding back as we know how we both feel. God my head hurts.

"Yeah, heard Kyle is turning every girl down now," Blonde one from last week says. Do they not look around them before they open their big mouths?

"Yeah saw it with my own eyes. Girls are throwing themselves at him and he just turns them down. I didn't have a chance to seduce him. I should've just gone for it when I had a chance." Blonde number two says. I can't help but smile knowing Kyle isn't continuing with the sluts at this school.

"I wanted him, now I lost my shot. Totally bummed. Last week he was all over any girl who approached him, this week he doesn't want anything to do with them. Strange." I roll my eyes. What girl talks like this?

"You think it's got to do with his ex?" I clear my throat and walk past them. I see them shut up and look anywhere but at me. I hate gossip unless Lex tells me it because I love seeing her face light up spilling on what scandals are happening in front of our noses.

I partnered up with Savannah, we talked about my parents. She never asked about Kyle or Derek, even though I know she is probably curious, but I appreciate she doesn't push. I want to fill her in about Kyle, but I have to stop thinking and wanting to talk about him. I have my goals and he's not on the list yet.

Lex meets up with me after school and drives us to the mall. I made a list of what to get my parents and Lex. I even thought of something to get James. He is part of Lex's life, which means he's part of mine. He's quiet around me, but the way he looks at Lex I know he adores her, maybe even loves her. We walk from one store to the next. My hands are full of bags, I think I went a little overboard. I walk past a jewelers and see something in the window that catches my eye.

"Lex?" I say stopping to look at the chain and pendant.

"Yeah, you need to get something else?" I nod and go inside the store. It's small, but the jewelry I do see is exquisite. I start looking at bracelets when a small old lady comes over asking if I need any help.

"Yes, please. Can I have a look at the chain with the circle pendant that's in the window?" I ask politely hoping she understands what I'm after.

"Of course. Let me get it for you," the lady opens the glass door that leads to the jewelry in the window. I turn and see Lex looking at the earrings. "This one?" The lady asks. I face her and look at the chain she has layed on a soft cushion. I pick it up gently and look at the circle pendant. I can't put my finger on it, but I know I need to get it. I know it belongs to Kyle. Have you ever got a present for someone just knowing it's for them? That's what this is. I know it's meant to be for Kyle.

"It's a St. Christopher necklace. Would you like to know its meaning?" I look up and nod my head. I feel Lex stand by my side taking a look at the necklace in my hands.

"The St. Christopher pendant is believed to protect its wearer, whether they are male or female. There is no variation in the design for either sex. The story goes that St. Christopher used to help people across a dangerous river, something that he was particularly good at due to his unique size and height. One day, he had to assist a child across the river and as he slowly waded through the water he noticed that the child became heavier with every step he took. St. Christopher actually started to struggle with the impossible weight of the small child that just kept increasing as he went on. Once he had finally gotten the child across he asked him why he was so heavy, completely baffled by the surprising weight. The child then revealed himself as a manifestation of Jesus Christ and replied that he had been so heavy as he carries the weight of the world's sins on his shoulders. As St. Christopher was successfully able to carry the burden of Christ across the river, he was entrusted as Protector of all Travelers."

"Wow, never realized a necklace can tell such a story," Lex says. I just nod my head. I like to know Kyle will be wearing it, it will be protecting him. Part of me feels like it's a double meaning to me. Kyle helping to carry my pain, my burden.

"I will take this, please. Thank you for sharing the story, it hits closer to home than I thought it would." I hand it over as the lady starts to put it in a box.

"Most pendants have some sort of meaning. I think this will make such a lovely gift." I pay for it and thank the lady again as I leave the store. I wasn't sure if I wanted to get presents for Kyle and Derek as I don't want to mislead them. If I got Kyle a gift, I need to Derek one. I will feel bad if I don't.

"That's for Kyle ain't it?" Lex asks eventually. I didn't realize we have been walking. God after hearing that story my head is a little out of it.

"Yeah, it is. When I saw it. I knew I had to get it for him."

"I understand. Kyle will love it."

"Thank you." I smile at Lex as we walk to few more stores. I finally get Derek a personalized drinking flask, knowing he uses one. It's not as meaningful as Kyle's, but I did put a little thought behind it. When it's time to head home, I feel relieved as my feet are killing me. I run for hours, and a little bit of shopping I'm ready to pass out on the couch in front of the TV.

When Lex drops me off at home, I give her a hug. When I step foot inside my home, I go straight to the couch and lay down dropping all my bags on the floor and not caring. I need a rest. I can't help but let out a loud moan. Don't think I can move a muscle.

"That bad huh," I pick my face up from the pillow and look up to see my dad sitting down on his recliner smiling at me. I can't help but smile back.

"My feet have decided to stop working. I can't move. Too much shopping," I groan again into the pillow. I hear my dad chuckle at me.

"Well looks like you bought the entire mall. What you did get me?" I don't get a chance to register what he just said as I hear him step towards me and peeking through my bags. I have to sit up and slap his hands away.

"Daddy, you have to wait till Christmas, no peeking." I grab the bags and pull them closer to me. Dad sits back down smiling at me.

"Least you moved now," I glare at him as he laughs at me, and I chuckle too. I missed this. "Got some news." I sit up when I notice his facial expression go serious. "We booked an appointment for you to see a therapist. She came very highly recommended. You will see her after school Friday, she will take it from there on what happens next." I know I needed help, but didn't think it would be this soon. Least I can get better sooner.

"Thanks for this Dad," I stand up and give him a hug, he hugs me back tightly.

"Just want you to be happy again." I smile at him.

"I will." I stand and take all my bags to my room. Hopefully, this therapist can help see what's wrong with me.

I look out my window and see Kyle taking some rubbish to the bins outside. I make a decision to have a word with him now. We need to stop blurring the lines. I need my friend back. Even though, the side he is showing me is so intense and turns me on so greatly. I need the Kyle that kept me at arm's length. I walk back downstairs and tell my parents I'm quickly running across to see Kyle and I will be back shortly. When I do walk to Kyle's door, I feel unsure. Do I walk in like I'm use to? Or knock? I decide to knock. I wait for him to answer.

When the door opens, Kyle is standing there with no top on. Does he walk around his house topless every day? I am staring at his hard toned abs and I just want to touch them. I feel like today at lunch was weeks ago and not just hours. I see his jeans resting on his hips, showing off his sexy V. God I have no coherent thought right now. I hear Kyle chuckle at me.

"See something you like baby girl?" I look up into Kyle's eyes and see the hunger pulling me in. I need to look away. I'm just finding it so hard to do that right now. I'm pretty sure I'm drooling right now.

"Ummm, we need to talk," I say, and my voice is a little shaky. I need to stay strong. Stupid hormones.

"Come in." Kyle opens the door wider, when I slide in I feel my breasts glide across Kyle's chest, causing me to gasp. I'm praying he didn't hear it. "What you want to talk about?" Kyle asks walking up the stairs towards his room. I can't go there. I know my mind will definitely turn to goo if I go in there.

"Can't we sit in the living room?"

"We always talk in my room. Unless you can't control yourself?" I hear the amusement in his voice. I feel the determination to prove him wrong, so I walk up the stairs and plunk myself on his bed. Resting my back against his headboard. I wish now I wasn't that stubborn. I see Kyle close his door, he turns and stares at me, causing my body to heat up. He walks over to his bed and crawls on it, facing me, then sits.

Dirty thoughts are corrupting my head.

"What you want Als?" That simple question has so much meaning. The words go straight between my thighs. I shake my head, trying to clear all lustful thoughts.

"We need to talk about our friendship." I see Kyle's eyes change from lustful to confusion to sadness. It takes all my will not to help take the sadness away. I know how to take it away, but I'm not ready for that. "Don't worry, we are staying friends, but it's how we been acting towards each other we need to talk about."

twenty-one

"What's wrong with how we act around each other? I like how we have been." I roll my eyes at him.

"We need to talk seriously, stop trying to make everything sound dirty. You need to stop dragging me into classrooms, closets, any sort of empty room. Friends don't act like that. We need to stay platonic. Can you do that?" I ask and look at him, he is trying not to smile at me.

"Come on, I never heard you complain once. I make you feel good, don't I? Do you know how hard it is to see you and not be able to touch you whenever I want? Every time I see you, I want to pin you against the closest wall and have my wicked way with you." Kyle says huskily, it takes so much will power to not react to his words.

"Kyle. We said friends. I need a friend right now. I need you to stop touching me, especially talking to me like you do. You need to be able to do this or we have to stay apart till I get things sorted. It's up to you." I hate that I have to give him an ultimatum, but I haven't got much choice.

"Fine." Fine? Fine what?

"Care to elaborate?"

"Fine, I won't cross any lines. We will go back to how we were.

I will control how my body wants to touch, feel and taste you." Kyle says slowly, and I feel the ache start to build, his words alone is causing me to get wet. How is that possible? "I want to stay in your life. I will be good." I look at him to make sure he means it. I see the sincerity in his eyes, so I know he is going to try.

"Thank you."

"Well, as we have to be good, want to watch a movie?" I can't help but smile. I missed our Friday nights. Even though it's not Friday, I need this.

"Sounds good." Kyle stands up and puts a DVD on, and comes and lays at my side. After a few minutes, "Jack and Jill" comes on. An Adam Sandler film. I smile knowing he has put it on for me. We lay next to each other watching the movie. I can feel the heat coming off him. I hate how he's not even touching me, not doing anything, and I'm aching for him. I want him to pin me against the bed. I told him we need to be good and I'm having impure thoughts.

"Als, want to sit at our table today?" Kyle asks. I look at Derek and he gives me a nod to say it's ok if I want to. I haven't sat with Kyle in ages. I need to make an effort with our friendship thing. Lex is happy that we are sitting here again. She is all googly eyes with James. "Thanks for sitting with me today," Kyle says.

"We are friends, no need to thank me. So any gossip?" I ask as I take a bite out of my sandwich.

"You want to hear gossip? Think you have spent too much time with Lex." I can't help but laugh.

"Heard that douche." Lex throws a fry at Kyle, it lands in his soup. I can't help but laugh louder.

"Babe, told you stop using my food for your food fights. Use yours." James complains moving his tray away from Lex, who rolls her eyes.

"I would, but lettuce wouldn't go far if I threw it."

"Then get your own fries, in case you need to make a point."

"Why would I do that as I have yours? You know that saying,

what's yours is mine, what's mine is mine." I can't help but giggle.

"Think it's, what's mine is ours and what's yours is ours." James corrects.

"Nah, I like my saying better." Lex grabs another fry and chucks it at Kyle, not moving her eyes from James, trying to make a point. James grabs her waist and starts tickling her, causing her to go into a fit of laughter. Everyone at the table is laughing and chuckling at them.

"It's like watching a soap opera with them two, very entertaining," Kyle says. And I laugh in agreement. I turn away from Lex and look at Kyle to see he is staring at me with a smile on his lips.

I look at him and see how handsome, how beautiful he is. His hair has grown longer, covering my view to his eyes. I run my fingers through his hair, feeling how soft it feels. I move his hair away and look into his eyes that are boring into mine. I don't know what causes me to do what I'm about to do, but I feel myself move closer to Kyle so that we are just a breath away. I lick my lips, accidentally touching his lip with my tongue, causing him to groan. That groan shutters my entire body.

I lean forward and when his lips touch mine, I feel like I'm home. I move my lips against his, it's pure heaven. The kiss is so slow and gentle. I think Kyle is afraid that I will push away any second. I don't want to. I want to keep going. I feel his tongue against my lips, I open my mouth, and I feel his tongue against mine. I can't help the moan that leaves me.

When I start to really get into the kiss, I feel someone grab me and pull me up. I feel a pain shoot through my back. I can't help the scream that leaves my throat. I feel the second stab. I look down at Kyle staring at me with pure horror in his eyes. He's trying to stand up, to get to me, it's like a force is keeping him away.

I feel someone's breath against my neck. I never felt so scared in my life. I feel eyes on me and see Caitlin standing a few feet away, watching me. Sadness all over her face. I can feel the breathing on my neck getting stronger. If Caitlin is in front of me, who is behind me? The not knowing is the scariest thing. I want to turn around, but

I can't. My body is stuck in the spot. I feel the knife get pulled out, causing me to scream again. I hear a chuckle behind me. Then I hear a whisper, causing goose bumps to cover my whole body.

"You are mine." I then feel the pain shoot through me again.

"Alison." I hear behind me. "Alison." "Alison." I wake up, shaking. I see Kyle at my side, holding me. My whole body is once again covered in sweat. Where am I? I look around to see that I'm still in Kyle's room. I must have fallen asleep watching the movie. My dreams are getting worse, they are scaring the shit out of me.

"You're ok, I'm here. I'm here. I'm never leaving you." Kyle says supporting words over and over. I don't know how long he holds me, but his hold loosens when he notices my body has calmed down. I feel so embarrassed that he had to witness that.

"Was that one of your nightmares?" Kyle asks, and I nod.

"Was it bad?"

"Yeah" I whisper. Kyle holds me again.

"That is the most terrifying thing I have ever heard. You were screaming and wouldn't stop. Just watching you like that."

"Lex said the same thing. My dad has got me a therapist, hoping that she will be able to help me. My nightmares are getting worse. It used to be Caitlin causing me the pain, now she just stands there, watching. It's someone else causing it, but I don't know who." Just talking about it gives me the shivers.

"God that sounds like a fucking horror movie, freaked out by just hearing you say it. Hopefully, the therapist can help get rid of the dreams. You can't live the rest of your life like that." I know I can't, I will go insane if I do. I will never want to go to sleep again.

"Feel like I'm in "A Nightmare on Elm Street" or something."

"Now that is a dream you never want to go in." I can't help but laugh.

"I'm sorry you witnessing that Kyle," I whisper.

"Don't be sorry. You are going through something. I hate how full on I have been. You said you are dealing with stuff, and I still came full on. It's me who needs to apologize. I'm here for you. In any way you want." Kyle grabs my hand and guides me to his lap. He holds me. Nothing sexual. Just a friend comforting a friend. We end up laying back down on the bed. Kyle eventually falls back to sleep. I can't help but watch him. He looks so peaceful. I'm glad I came here. We may not be able to go back, but we can make a new start. I hear my phone vibrate on the floor. I quickly dislodge myself from Kyle without waking him and pick up my phone, noticing I have some message from Derek.

Derek: Hey, wondering if you fancy pizza night with a comedy on Saturday? Don't worry no alcohol involved ;)

Derek: Just text me when you get this. Worried about you x

Derek: Heading to sleep now. Hope you're ok x

I feel bad that he was worried. I look over at Kyle and down at the message about Saturday. Why do I feel like I'm doing something wrong? Kyle knows I'm friends with Derek. We are friends, nothing more. I reply back to Derek.

Me: Sorry, fell asleep. Yeah, Saturday sounds good, can't wait. Heading back to sleep. See you tomorrow at school x

Just a few seconds later I get a reply.

Derek: Was starting to really worry, glad you're ok. Looking forward to Sat. See you tomorrow x

I don't reply back. I lay back down and stare at the ceiling. I can't fall back to sleep, it's too late to run. I feel so frustrated about it. I decide that I need to go back to my house. I get a pen and paper from Kyle's desk and leave him a note that I couldn't sleep and headed home, no need to worry. When I got home, everything was quiet, my parents must have gone to bed already. I have a quick shower and decide to read on my Kindle. Hoping to eventually fall back to sleep, or wait till sun starts to rise so I can go for a run. Either way works for me.

twenty-two

Kyle and I have fallen back to our normal routine. Kyle messaged Lex that he is going back to picking us both up from and to school. Since Tuesday night, Kyle hasn't once took advantage of a situation with me. He has been a perfect gentleman. When he asked me on Thursday if I wanted to join him at his table for lunch, I had to decline as it reminded me so much of my dream, I couldn't do it. I hated seeing the disappointment that I said no in his eyes. When I sat next to Derek, talking about Saturday, I couldn't help but look at Kyle at his table watching him look down. I hate that I'm the cause of it.

It's officially Friday, the day I see my therapist. Three days away till Caitlin's hearing, last day of school for Christmas. I have been a bucket full of nerves since I woke up. My parents have told me to just say what's on my mind, that I shouldn't hold anything back. I'm not worried about me talking about everything that's happened, I'm worried that she isn't able to help me, cure me. What if I have to suffer from these nightmares for life? I know I shouldn't think it, but I can't help it.

"Come on, sit with me." I hear Kyle say grabbing my hand. Guiding me to his table.

"What are you doing?" I feel a little panicky.

"I've watched you stare at your drink for ten minutes. You are sitting next to me, I'm going to help make you laugh. Forget about you know what." I sigh and let him guide me into my seat. I look over at Derek's table to see him look at me. I see anger written all over his face. I quickly text him to say I was feeling nervous about seeing my therapist today, Kyle is trying to cheer me up. I see him look at his phone, see his posture relax. Don't know why he looked angry but least it looks like he has calmed down now.

"Finally. I missed this table. Only so much Tom I can handle." Lex says as she plunks down in her chair.

"Yeah, Tom is a little up himself," I reply back.

"A little? He thinks he's God's gift. So glad I'm taking a breather from him."

"Yo Lex Legs, feel heartbroken you have dissed me," Tom yells over the cafeteria, causing Lex to groan. James laughs.

"Hey, you shouldn't be laughing at that weasel. You should be wanting to kick his ass for talking to me like that." Lex hits James arm, and I can't help but laugh at them.

"Come on, it's Tom. If I hit him, it's like hitting a puppy." James says.

"Tom is now a puppy? He's a pervert," Lex groans.

"A perverted puppy," someone says down the table, we all laugh.

"Lex, I miss you, baby," Tom yells again, this time I can't help but laugh, so I hide my face in Kyle's shoulder.

"Fuck you, Tom." Lex groans.

"Any time, any place, hot lips."

"Grrrr, someone please gag him. Of all things holy."

Kyle drives me to my therapist appointment. I told him I didn't mind walking as it's twenty minutes away from the school, but he insisted. I'm now sitting in the car, looking at the huge glass style building. Why am I so nervous? I just sit there and talk, she listens. No big deal. I feel Kyle's hands interlaced with mine. I feel his strength for me flow through me. I can do this.

"I will pick you up in an hour. No complaints," Kyle quickly says before I have a chance to interrupt. "After, movie and Chinese at mine. We need to get our Friday night traditions back on track.

"Sounds great. God, why am I so nervous?"

"You're going to meet a complete stranger and give every gory detail on what you are going through. You have to relive what happened and retell your dreams. It's going to be tough. But remember you're a strong person."

"I don't feel strong," I say quietly, looking again at the building,

"It takes a strong person to ask for help. You can do this." Kyle leans over and kisses my cheek, I feel my cheeks flush. That little contact, I felt it all over my body.

"See you in an hour." I get out of the car and head towards the posh looking building. When I get to the glass door, I turn around and see Kyle still in his car, watching me, making sure I get inside all right. I take a deep breath and push the door open.

The whole place looks brand new. Everything looks immaculate. I walk forward seeing a reception desk. When I get there, a blonde girl who looks a few years older than me greets me with a soft smile.

"Hi, welcome to Campbell offices, how can I help you?"

"Hi, I have an appointment under Alison McCartney." I feel my throat get dry so I have to cough a couple of times. I need to control these nerves.

"Just one second," the receptionist says as she goes through the computer. "Ok go to the elevator on the right and press three. There will be a seating area to your left. Just wait there and Mrs. Pruitt will be with you shortly."

"Thank you." I follow the directions and sit on a black leather couch. I look around me and see some doors that must lead to the therapist rooms. I look down the hallway that is on the right-hand side and wonder what's down there. I see few magazines on the coffee table in front of me and decide to flick through. It's what you do when waiting for appointments. You look through pictures of magazines reading the odd article. I've been waiting probably five minutes when I hear my name being called. I look up seeing a woman who looks to be in her forties, same height as me, wearing jeans and a light blue blouse. Don't know what I was expecting, but thought she would be wearing a suit or something.

"Hi, welcome Alison, my name is Mrs. Pruitt, you can call me Janine if that makes you feel more comfortable," Janine says shaking my hand, guiding me to a chair. Thought I would be lying down like you see in the movies, but guess not. She has a desk with pictures of her family all over the walls, some drawings from kids. Think it's meant to help make this place feel more homely.

"Hi, Janine." Janine gives me a smile, glad I'm using her first name.

"Well, your father told me you want someone to talk to. He gave me details on your situation. I'm here to listen and help in any way that I can. Whatever you tell me here doesn't leave this office. First off, to start out slow, tell me a little about yourself." I look at her, seeing her comforting eyes. I feel at ease here. I know I need to do this, to help me move on. Help the nightmares go away.

"Well, I'm seventeen, eighteen in April. I love to read and watch movies. I enjoy running. When I run, it helps clear my mind. I have loving parents. Two best friends. Guess I gained a few more friends in the past couple of months. I had a boring life till a few months ago.

"What happened a few months ago?" Janine asks.

"Well, I was invisible. My two best friends were popular, noticed. Lex, my best friend, took me to a spa and I had a little makeover. Then after that my life started to change. Boys were noticing me. Even Kyle started to notice me."

"Kyle?"

"My other best friend."

"But he is something more than a best friend?"

"Yeah, he was. I had a crush on him as long as I could remember. He protected me. Was always there for me. Before the incident happened, we got together."

"You're not together now?"

"No, after what happened, we started growing distant from each other, we were both dealing with what happened differently. We pushed each other away. I ended it, feeling it was for the best."

"Do you still believe that? That it was for the best?"

"Yeah I do. We needed space. Because we did give each other space, we found each other again. We decided we want to be in each other's lives even if we are just friends.

"That's very mature. Most teenagers would treat the situation more dramatically." I can't help but laugh.

"Trust me, I did things that weren't acted out from maturity. I drank twice to the point I passed out. I took everything out on my parents. I hit a girl who thought she would be my new bully."

"People drink when they experience something so traumatic. It's a normal response. Normal again to take it out on the ones you love. With hitting the girl, what do you mean new bully? You have been bullied before?" I explain everything about Savannah, from when we were kids, to what she was like before Caitlin to how she is now.

"Seems like she feels guilty for what's she's done. She probably even feels a little responsible for what happened. The things that go on in people's minds, especially if they feel like they were involved at all. You said she admitted to vandalizing your locker, she probably thought that her doing that was getting back at what Caitlin was doing. If she didn't spray-paint your locker, would Caitlin been caught sooner?"

"Never thought of it like that. She has stuck up for me. Help defend me."

"She's trying to make amends. Like I said, situations like these make you think twice about your life." We kept talking, we talked about Derek, Caitlin, the Halloween party, to the incident, to my nightmares. Soon as I opened up I couldn't stop, every question Janine asked, I answered.

"So how do I get the nightmares to stop?" I pleadingly ask.

"Seems to me your nightmares went from your normal traumatic issues being played out. You were worried Kyle would have chosen Caitlin over you. Him going to Savannah. It was your insecurities mixed into what happened, you blaming yourself, even without you realizing it."

"What you mean?"

"You probably thought what if you didn't have your makeover? Would Kyle still want a relationship? Would he have ended up with Caitlin otherwise? It's the what ifs. You probably even thought, would you have done the same thing as Caitlin? You did love Kyle from a young age." she's right, I remember thinking that when I was returning back to school.

"Now the nightmares look like they are trying to tell you something, without you realizing it. Caitlin was the cause, but now she isn't the one doing the harming. The question is, who is?" That question alone sends goosebumps all over. "I think if you find out who it is the nightmares should stop, or ease off."

"So I have to figure out who the person behind me is?" Janine nods. Great, I have to go into nightmare land and deal with another lunatic.

"Another thing. Are you going to the hearing on Monday?" How does she know about the hearing? "Your father told me, like I said he told me a little summary so I knew what to expect."

"Well, I don't know. I want to, but I'm scared to go. Just seeing her, don't think I'm ready."

"I know it's hard. It's facing your demons. I think it would do you good though. Maybe even help get closure. Just think about it."

"I will."

"Ok, well our hour is up. . . I think we covered a fair amount of ground. It's up to you if you want to come back. If you do just tell your father to set up another appointment. If not then I wish you the best. It's good that you decided to get help. Most people wouldn't. It's a brave thing."

"Kyle said the same thing."

"Smart man." I can't help but laugh.

"At times." I know I want another appointment. I want to make sure I'm mentally stable before I stop. I say my goodbyes and when I leave the building I feel better. Like more weight has left my shoulders. I know it's going to take time, but I feel like I know I'm going to be ok. I look up and see Kyle leaning against his car, legs crossed, arms crossed. He is watching me. God that guy is sin on a stick. He's definitely my weakness.

twenty-three

"How did it go?" Kyle asks after a while. When I walked to him after my appointment, he held me. He didn't ask or say anything, he just held me. I relaxed into his arms, not wanting to go anywhere but here. Guess he wants to make sure I'm ok.

"We talked about everything, from beginning of the school year to now. She said some stuff that I never thought twice about. I am going to see her again. She is so nice and she never once judged me or felt sorry for me. I needed this, glad I went." I ramble on. Now that I started talking from my session can't stop.

"I'm so happy that it went great. You do seem happier already. If you don't mind me asking, what did she say about the nightmares?" I explained to him what Janine said. "Makes sense. I just hate that you have to go through all that. I know it's a dream, but for you to feel that pain and see who is causing it. Wish I could do it for you." I smile at him and see his face torn with pain for me. I put my hand in his as he drives like we use to.

"I know. Was thinking as well, might go to the hearing on Monday. I need to find closure, and if I can get it by hearing what Caitlin has to say, I have to do it."

"Do you think that's a good idea? You sure you're ready?" Kyle says, quickly looking at me then facing the road again.

"I need to try, if not, I'm always going to wonder what if. I need to stop the what ifs and face my problems."

If that's what you want, then I'm with you." We talk more about my session till I hear my phone ding telling me I got a message.

Derek: How did it go? You ok? If you need to talk, I'm here x

Me: It went better than what I thought. I'm ok, still processing everything she said, but I think this will do me good. With Kyle at the moment, but will talk tomorrow. Thank you for thinking of me x

Maybe I shouldn't have said I was with Kyle. I need to stop thinking like this. I'm not going to hide what I'm doing when I'm with one of them.

Derek: Least you're not alone. I'll see you tomorrow x

Me: See you tomorrow x

"Lex checking up on you?" I really want to groan, I always feel the guilt when I talk about the other to the person I'm with.

"No, Derek, just checking that I'm ok."

"Nice of him," Kyle says tightly.

"Yeah, it was. So what movie are we watching?" I asked trying to change the subject.

"See what you did there. I'll let you pick."

"What did I do?" I flutter my eyelashes, trying to look innocent.

"You know you changed the subject on purpose."

"Who? Me? Never." I can't help but laugh. "You sure you are trusting me to pick the movie?"

"Don't make me take it back." Kyle jokes.

"No, just checking. Know what film to pick on as well." I rub my hands acting like I'm an evil villain.

"Oh God, it's going to be a chick flick ain't it?" Kyle groans.

"You will see." I do the evil laugh, causing Kyle to laugh.

"I should've known you would make me watch a pansy ass film," Kyle groans out load when David Bowie starts to sing.

"The Labyrinth is a classic, besides, I think David Bowie is hot in this film," I shrug eating another piece of popcorn.

"You think a man wearing tight ass trousers that shows his bulge is sexy?" He asks in disbelief.

"I never really noticed his package, but showing concern that you were looking." I can't help but laugh from the look on Kyle's face.

"How can you not notice it? It's in your face."

"I enjoy the storyline and the catchy music." I start to sing along with David Bowie. "What kind of magic spell do you use? Slime and snails, or puppy dogs tails. Thunder or lightning? Then baby said dance, magic, dance..."

"Oh God, please stop, the words don't even make sense."

"Dance, magic dance, jump magic jump." I keep singing. I'm standing on Kyle's bed doing my own little dance moves.

"No more." Next thing I know I've been pulled down on the bed, Kyle is on top of me tickling me. "You going to stop singing that stupid song?" I look at him and I can't help but laugh then continue singing the words. Kyle tickles me so much that I can't form words.

"Stop, please stop," I say between laughter.

"You going to stop singing?"

"I won't sing anymore of this song." Kyle starts to ease away from me. "But not promising on the future songs." I laugh again as Kyle falls on top of me, putting all his weight on me. "God Kyle you weigh as much as a house."

"Did warn you." He hums. He's bloody humming, I can't breathe in.

"I can't breathe, you big buffoon."

"You have to promise not to sing along with this dreadful, awful movie you are punishing me with." Because I need air, I agree. Kyle lifts his chest, I gulp loads of air in.

"God, thought I was going to pass out. You big brute."

"I love it when you talk dirty." I can't help but laugh. When I look at him, he's still on top of me. I realized he is in between my legs. Don't ask me, but I move my hips a little and moan when I feel the contact.

"Als, I can't do what you asked if you do things like that," Kyle says gruffly. I give up fighting to stay away from him. He wants me, I know I want him, even my body is craving him. He has been there for me. No one can ever replace Kyle, he's part of me. I make the decision. I want him. I want him to be my friend as well as my lover.

"I changed my mind, I'm sorry Kyle, but I want you, I need you. Can we be more than friends again?" I look into Kyle's eyes and feel worried that maybe Kyle doesn't want to start up a relationship with me, maybe he just wanted a little bit of fun with no strings attached. Before my mind thinks of worse scenarios, his lips are on mine.

"You have me, you always have. I won't ruin it this time. You sure this is what you want?" I see the uncertainty that maybe he thinks I will change my mind.

"I'm sure, it's always been you, Kyle." With that, Kyle's lips are back on mine, they are full of hunger and want. He starts to grind against me. I wrap my legs around him, pulling him closer to me. God this feels so incredible. Why did I ever deny myself of this? I'm so turned on, I can feel the wetness between my legs.

"I missed this," Kyle growls into my ear, making my whole body shiver.

"It's only been a few days." I breathe out.

"No, I missed owning this body. Hated that we had to go back to where I wanted you, but couldn't touch you. Never letting you go again." I can't help but feel the warmth that the words bring.

"I'm yours."

"Your mine," Kyle growls again. I feel him getting harder if that's even possible. Kyle unbuttons my jeans and slides them along my legs. I feel his hands trail up my bare legs till he reaches my lace underwear. I can't help but arch into his hands. I feel him pull the material aside and slip a finger through my folds. I groan by the contact. "You're so perfect, so beautiful."

"Kyle, please," I beg. I need this release. I need him to give me more. My eyes are closed tight, and when I feel a warmth slide through my wetness, I open my eyes to see Kyle has his tongue on me. I watch with half-lidded eyes. No one has ever gone down on me. I should feel embarrassed, but I'm not. It feels so good. When Kyle sucks on my clit, I yell out. My legs are shaking, I feel the ache get so strong and the next thing I know I'm screaming Kyle's name as I let everything go.

"Knew you would taste like heaven," Kyle smiles down at me, I didn't notice him move up the bed.

"That was amazing." Kyle chuckles.

"I'm glad you liked it." God I bloody loved it. Never knew it could be like that.

"I more than liked it." I'm still so turned on. I move so I'm straddling Kyle's legs. I help him out of his jeans, and when I release him from his boxers, I see how hard he really is. I see a little moisture on the tip, I lean forward and lick it off, causing Kyle to groan. I never have actually done this so I take my time. I lick him from top to base, then I put him fully in my mouth. He is so big that I have to use my hand to help. I see Kyle grasping onto the sheets. I feel myself getting wet all over again.

"Fuck, so good. So fucking good," Kyle gasps out.

I want him inside me, I want him to be my first. He was meant to take my virginity on the night of the Halloween dance. My mind is so full of lust and want. I sit up but never once let go of Kyle's cock. His eyes are closed. I get into position then I slowly ease down, guiding Kyle inside me. I feel so full, with one quick motion I push down quickly, causing me to scream, and Kyle to scream in pleasure.

"Als, fuck," Kyle sits up and wraps his arms around me. "Why did you do that?" Kyle is breathing so heavy, I feel my inner muscles tighten. "Fuck, you're squeezing me." Kyle pants into my shoulder. Neither of us has moved. I knew it would hurt, but never thought it would be like this. I feel so damned full. I can't move, even if I wanted to.

"I wanted you inside me, I need you, Kyle. But it hurts, I don't think I can move," I whisper, I feel so embarrassed. This should be good for him and I'm messing it up.

"Baby, you just gave me your virginity. I would have eased you into it. Let me help make it feel good." I nod, and Kyle flips us over so I'm laying on my back, with us still connected together. "I'm going to move slowly, you should've got used to me by now. I'll go really slowly." I can only nod again. I feel Kyle ease out, then push back in. After few thrusts, it starts to feel pleasurable.

Kyle must have such control as he keeps going at his slow pace, it's gone to the point it's driving me crazy. I need him to go faster. I start to move my hips with him and it hits the right angle that I moan into Kyle's shoulder. I push my heels into Kyle's ass, helping him move faster. Kyle finally takes the hint. He starts to speed up watching for my reaction, when he sees only pleasure, he goes harder. I can't help but scream out his name. God it feels so good. I never want this to stop. Kyle keeps going. Then his thumb is on my clit and starts to rub, I explode. After few more thrusts, Kyle comes with me.

"Fuck, so tight, so good," Kyle says into my neck. We lay like that for what feels like hours, but Kyle eventually gets up and walks to his bathroom. He comes back out with a wet cloth.

"Open your legs, baby," I love that he is calling me baby, but I feel too embarrassed to comply. We just made love and I feel embarrassed. "I just want to clean you up." The words are so soft that I open my legs When the cloth hits my sensitive area I wince, never realized how tender it feels down there. Kyle puts the cloth away and lays next to me on the bed, he guides my head on his chest and starts to stroke my hair.

"Thank you for giving me your precious gift."

"It was always yours Kyle, I always wanted it to be you," I say giving his chest a little kiss.

"I love you Als," I look up, looking into his eyes I can't help the tears that fall from my eyes by just seeing so much love shine from him.

"I love you Kyle, always have." Kyle uses his thumb to dry away my tears and kisses my forehead.

"I'm sorry about Caitlin. I hate how I was towards women. Never thought of the consequences. I wanted you. I thought I never stood a chance. I should've been more patient. Do you forgive me?" I look at him again, resting my head looking into his eyes, I knew I already have, didn't know when I stopped blaming him, but I have.

"Already have," I get a warm smile in return, we both fall asleep. That night I had no nightmares.

twenty-four

I wake up in Kyle's arms feeling at peace with the world. I had the best sleep I had in months. One thing I'm happy about is that I had no nightmares, maybe I was emotionally exhausted? But hope they don't come back anytime soon. I reach over to grab my phone from the side table next to me and groan when I see the time. After 10 a.m. already. I haven't slept in this long since the nightmares started. I stand up and I feel a little tenderness between my legs, and can't help but smile, knowing Kyle was there. I had sex, I, Alison McCartney, had sex with Kyle Jacobs.

I quickly use the toilet, then wash my hands, when I look at my reflection, I was hoping to see a change. I look the same. My cheeks are a little flush, but that's from the sleep. Oh well, least my parents won't be able to tell. When I go back to Kyle's room, he's sitting up against the headboard. I see his bare chest and all I want to do is go over there and touch him slowly all over, but I made plans with Derek. I start to get redressed and before I know it, I'm being pinned down on the bed.

"You know, you need to stop dragging me around like a rag doll," I say in laughter. I sigh when I feel Kyle's lips against mine.

"I will try to remember that." He continues to kiss me, after few minutes, I have to push him away even though I could stay like this for hours.

"I need to head home and shower, have plans for later." I stand up putting my shoes on.

"Plans with Lex?" Kyle asks, and already I hate that I have to mention Derek.

"No, not Lex." I quickly put on my other shoe so I can run out of here before Kyle loses it. Don't get a chance, Kyle pulls me against his chest and holds me tightly.

"Who you have plans with babe?" Kyle starts to kiss up my neck, I feel his heat from his chest against my back, God I hate how my mind is melting away.

"Derek," I whisper, I feel Kyle tense up.

"Derek?" I nod. "I don't like this Als." I look at him, he has fire in his eyes, I start to glare at him, and I'm not losing a friend, especially one who was there when he started to fool around with other girls. I need to move past it, I know it, but he has no right when it comes to my friendship with Derek.

"Well, Derek is my friend, he was there when you weren't. I'm not going to stop our friendship because you don't like it. I'm afraid you have to deal with it," I turn around and face him, showing him I'm serious.

"Right, fine. Your right, he was there when I wasn't. Just don't like it, but I will cope with it," he says tensely.

"Thank you," I kiss his cheek and open his door. I need to go shower, I have a feeling I smell like sex and bed. I start walking down the stairs and when I get to the front door, I feel Kyle turn me around and pin me against the door. His mouth slams down on me, it's no-where near gentle. I'm sure my lips are going to be red and swollen, but right now I don't care, I kiss him with everything I got.

"Just wanted to kiss you goodbye," Kyle helps my legs back on the ground. When did I wrap myself around him?

"Some goodbye," I say breathlessly.

"Just wanted you to remember you're my girl. Text me ok, just let me know you're safe," I roll my eyes at him. "Just do it for me." I agree, we kiss gently for a few minutes, I leave and head back to mine. The first thing I notice is the for sale sign on the front. I freeze, this is really happening. I take a deep breath, and walk past it and head inside.

"Mom, Dad, I'm home," I yell out.

"We're in the kitchen," Mom yells out. I walk towards them, don't want to be around them for too long as don't want them to sense what Kyle and I got up to last night.

"Hi Princess, how was your sleepover?" I blush.

"Yeah, fell asleep watching the movie. No nightmares, just literally woke up thirty minutes ago."

"That's great news, how did your session go? You wanting to go again?" Mom asks, leaning against the kitchen counter. I explain everything that went on and told them I do want to see Janine again. Mom and Dad are happy that I slept without any nightmares, they are acting like I won the lottery or something.

"I'll make a follow-up appointment then," Dad says.

"We also discussed Caitlin's hearing and I've decided to go. I need to try and get some closure." I look at both my parents and I see them trying to process what I said.

"You sure sweetie? If it's what you want, we will back you. I just know it's going to be hard seeing her in person, especially after your nightmares."

"I know, but I think I need this. I will regret it if I don't. If it gets too hard, I will leave."

"Ok, we will go with you. Just hate it's so close to Christmas. Who plans hearings this close to Christmas day?" Mom complains. I tell them I need to go have a shower. Least that went easier than what I thought.

I have a long shower, then start to get ready to head to Derek's. I need to tell him Kyle and I are giving it another go. I know he is going to be upset. We shared a kiss, just hope he wasn't hoping we were going to get together eventually or something. I shake my head and tell myself to have fun with Derek, he's my friend, he's going to be happy for me. Well, that's what I keep saying over and over. I tell my parents I'm heading to Derek's to watch a movie, they both look at me with confusion.

"You're going to Derek's?" Mom asks.

"Yes, I won't be out too late," I say hoping they feel relieved that I will be coming back home.

"What about Kyle?" Dad asks. I never asked what plans Kyle had. I should've asked. What if he is going to a party like he normally does on a Saturday? I need to trust him.

"Told him I'm going to see Derek, we are friends, Kyle gets that."

"Oh ok," Mom says feeling a little disappointed. Why is she upset?

"If it makes you feel any better, Kyle and I are giving it another go, but Derek has been a good friend to me, I can't just stop talking to him." I see the smiles on my parents faces. God they are just happy I'm not ending back with Derek.

"You should've said, have fun, will see you when you get back home," Dad says, I roll my eyes at him. I say my goodbyes, and head out the door. I see Kyle leaning against his car. He is wearing a tight black top that shows how toned his body is and black jeans with black army boots. He looks so delicious. Part of me wants to cancel with Derek and just spend more time with Kyle. I know I wouldn't though, I wouldn't cancel with a friend just to hook up with her boyfriend. Boyfriend, I can't help but smile thinking Kyle is my boyfriend again. Mine.

"Waiting for someone?" I ask when I get closer to Kyle.

"You. I knew you needed a ride, so I'm going to take you." I can't help but smile. He has been waiting for me to help give me a lift. Just makes me want him more.

"You didn't have to, was going to get a bus."

"I'm happy to, now get your cute little butt in. Sooner you spend time with him, sooner I know you are in your warm bed." I can't help but chuckle at him. Kyle drives me to Derek's. I didn't have to tell him where to go, he just knew. Derek must have thrown a party before. When we arrive, Kyle tells me to text him that I'm ok. I explain that he took me here, that I got here safely, but he still wants me to text him, so I just agree. I kiss him quickly on the lips and get out of the car. I stand there and wait till he drives off. I then turn and head for Derek's door. I ring the doorbell and wait. It didn't take long for Derek to answer.

"Wow, you look amazing," Derek smiles at me. I can't help but smile back. He is wearing a white shirt, rolled up at his shoulders and a pair of dark blue jeans. He looks great as well.

"Thanks, so do you." Derek opens the door, and I walk inside. We walk towards the living room. I appreciate that we aren't going to his room.

"Pizza is on the way, remember you saying you love Adam Sandler films so got quite a few options for you to choose from."

"Awww, thank you." I walk towards the glass coffee table and sit on the floor as I go through the collection. I decide on the Wedding Singer. Derek puts it in, we sit on the couch and watch the movie as we wait for the pizza. Twenty minutes later the pizza arrives, I can't help but eat three slices, one after the other.

"Hungry?" I can't help but laugh. I bet I don't look attractive eating like a cavewoman.

"Yeah sorry, I eat like a guy when I'm hungry." Derek laughs with me.

"Least you enjoy eating. Hate girls who starve themselves."

"Love food too much. Good thing I run, it helps burn all the food I do eat."

"You do have a great figure," Derek says checking me out, and I can't help but feel a little uncomfortable about it. Only because I know I'm with Kyle now and he wouldn't like how Derek is drinking me in.

"Thank you," I say and continue to watch the movie. I feel my phone vibrate in my pocket, I take it out and read a text from Kyle.

Kyle: Where was my text that you are safe? You could be tied to a chair for all I know.

I can't help but roll my eyes.

Me: Sorry I forgot. I'm not tied up, just eating pizza, watching wedding singer x

Kyle: Better you than me. Glad you're ok though, miss you x x

Me: You just don't appreciate good movies, miss you, too x x

Kyle: Msg me in an hour ok, just so I know you're still ok x x

Me: Fine, I will x x

Kyle: Don't forget x x

Me: I won't x x

Kyle: Love you x x

I can't help but feel the flutter from just reading the words, I can't help but smile.

Me: Love you, too x x

"What's making you smile so much?" Derek asks. I look at him, I know I need to tell him about me and Kyle.

"Kyle and I are giving it another go, he was just checking up on me." I watch Derek and he has a look of confusion.

"When did this happen?"

"Last night, we talked and I can't deny what we feel for each other. We love each other." I start to see Derek's eyes turn angry and I start feel very uncomfortable.

"What? He screwed around with other girls, you give him another chance?" Derek starts to raise his voice.

"He never actually slept with anyone," I quietly say, Derek is shaking his head. Didn't think he would take this so badly.

"I didn't sleep with Savannah. What we did, I was drunk and you couldn't forgive me. Kyle has been messing around with other girls, sober, and he gets you back. He may not be fucking other girls, but trust me, he has done everything but. Girls have been flaunting it about how good his tongue is." Derek spits out at me. I look at him with pure shock that he would say that to me.

"We weren't together, doesn't matter now. We are together. I'm sorry you are hurting over this, but we can still be friends, don't want to lose you. You've been good to me."

"Friends, I wanted to be more than fucking friends. You said you were dealing with shit. I knew you weren't ready. After two weeks, two fucking weeks, you took him back. So much for dealing with your fucked up head." Derek stands up, I look up at him, this is first time I have seen an ugly side to Derek.

"Derek, please calm down, you're scaring me." I plead.

"Scaring you? You have any idea what I went through to get you to come to me again? You are meant to belong to me. We look good together, you are a good person. You are part of my future plan, you are FUCKING IT UP!" I can't help but stand up and take a few steps away from him.

twenty-five

I'm looking at Derek pulling his hair as he walks back and forth. I don't know what to do, I want to run out the door, but afraid if I even try, something bad will happen. I need to text Kyle to get me, but how? I can't believe Derek is acting like this. He has always seemed normal.

"Fuck, you really love him?" Derek asks, and I nod. "Fuck, this isn't supposed to happen. I thought I lost my chance after what Caitlin had done, thought you and Kyle would be inseparable, but lucky for me, you both pushed each other away. Now, NOW, you both decide after a couple of stupid weeks, to give it another go." Derek is staring at me, and I push further against the wall, hoping it would eat me up.

"I have been there for you. Listened to you go on and complain about your life. I helped you, what do you do? Throw it in my face. I tried to push you both away before, you never took the hint then either, now you saw what Kyle was doing to every girl at school, and yet you crawl back to him." He tried to push us both away before? Does he mean when he acted all possessive and drove me home instead of Kyle? I know deep down that's not what he meant.

"What do you mean I never took the hint?" I whisper. Derek faces me and I see him smirk at me.

"The letters, remember those? I told you, warned you to stay away. You didn't listen." Derek wrote the letters, but Caitlin did them. I remember my parents telling me how she denied about the letters, photos, and dog. Oh my God, Derek did them all.

"You did the letters, photos and the umm, the umm," I can't even finish the sentence. I see the dog brutalized on my bed.

"Yeah, all me. Savannah being so stupid vandalizing your locker, took the heat off me. Couldn't plan that bit better myself, then the whole Caitlin thing, God it definitely took the blame away from me. They just pinned it all on her. She had an insane moment, a screw loose moment. I thought I lost my chance with you, really thought you both would have been stronger than ever, but thank my lucky stars I had a second chance." He sounds crazy. He did it all. Caitlin just had a stupid set back. I can't process all this.

"But why?"

"Why? WHY? I told you my parents have set my future in stone, I needed a future partner, a perfect person to be my side. I saw you, looking all stunning, I sensed the vulnerability, the innocence roll off you. You would look amazing on my arm. You are kind, sweet, who wouldn't want that in their life. I even started to fall for you. I could sense though that part of you belonged to Kyle. I tried to throw all my attention at you. One night, one stupid night, Savannah had to take me when I was feeling low. So when the police came sniffing about, I planted photos around her house. Wasn't hard. The police saw that and threw it all at her. Served the bitch right. With how she treated you, they thought they had their man then. Police are stupid, throw a little evidence around and they think their job is done, stupid." He planned everything. I start to feel my legs go weak, and I slide down the wall.

"Derek, please just let me go," I beg. A few tears are starting to slide down my cheek.

"I can't let you go, don't you see? You are it for me. I can't let you go." My whole body shakes just hearing him say the words. He isn't going to let me go. Derek starts pacing again. I watch him, and with one hand I feel for my phone in my pocket, I just need to ring Kyle and hope he can hear me. I see it done in the movies all the time, it has to work. I press the phone on, thankfully I haven't got the one you need to enter a code. I press the number 1 and press call, hoping I pressed everything correctly. I can just hear the ringing tone, hoping Derek can't hear it from when he's standing. Then I hear Kyle's voice, this is it. Please hear me, Kyle.

"So you're never letting me go. You are just going to keep me against my will, hoping I spend my future with you? Do you know how stupid that sounds? You need to let me go, please let me go," I cry and scream the last part, hoping Kyle heard it, even if it's just the last part.

"DON'T YELL AT ME! I'm thinking. This is so messed up, this isn't how it's meant to go. Caitlin was meant to be with Kyle or with some slut, you are meant to be with me. That's how it should've been. The poor girl was in love with Kyle, she listened to him, was there for him, like I have for you. What do you both do? You threw it in our faces. You fuck up with people. No wonder she had a bad judgment call." Derek sneers at me.

"What's your excuse for doing that thing to the dog, how could you do that?" I cry.

"I just meant to hurt the dog, but I saw the photos of you and Kyle and the anger took over, you know what it's like where the anger takes over. I see it in your eyes with Trina. From what you told me about yelling at your parents. The anger was consuming you, I helped you pull away from it. I know what anger does.

"I would never hurt a poor living thing. You're just sick in the head."

"Maybe I am. Maybe I'm thinking this because of the pressures my family put on me. Maybe it's due to not being loved enough, who knows. But you were meant to help me be better, but you fucked it up. Maybe I need to do a Caitlin." I look up and see Derek walk into the kitchen. I hear him open a drawer. Out of instinct, I run to the door, I run with everything in me. When the door is finally open, I get pulled back by my hair, I scream from the pain. Derek wraps his arms around me, pinning me to him. I feel his breath on my neck. I have a sense of Deja vu.

"Where the fuck do you think you're going?" Derek hisses at me, and he chucks me on the floor. I crawl back against the wall. I watch Derek pick up a knife, my whole body tightens up. Is he going to stab me? I can't go through all that again.

"Don't worry love, this ain't for you. This is for the piece of shit who has to fuck up everything." I know he means Kyle, oh no he is going to hurt Kyle. How does he know Kyle is coming? "I watched you dig in your pocket, thought you could get away with that without me noticing? Guess he should be here any minute, think it's his turn to feel what you went through. What was it? Two stabs in the back? Think it slides in like butter?" I look at Derek, watching the knife. How could I have hung out with Derek, talked to him, sat with him at lunch and not sense this? I guess you never really know what goes through people's head. Look at Caitlin, straight A student, with a bright future.

"Derek, please. Don't do this." I cry for what is going to happen. I can't watch this, I can't watch Derek hurt Kyle. I lived, what if Kyle doesn't?

"Too late, need to do this, haven't got a choice." Derek stands near the door, waiting. I sit there, trying to think what to do. He saw me getting to my phone so I can't do it again without him noticing. I then hear a car screech to a stop. Oh no, it's Kyle. Please, Kyle, don't come in, please don't come in. I sit there frozen from what I'm about to see. I see Kyle look through windows, I know he sees me. I don't have a chance to signal him not to come in. He's gone. I hear him bang on the door. No, please, no. As soon as the door opens I run towards Derek. I bang into him as soon as he raises the knife. Derek falls against the wall, we both start to fight for the knife. I'm digging my nails into his hands trying to get him to loosen up his grip. Kyle seems frozen for a second when he sees the knife in Derek's hands, then he has joined in trying to get the knife away.

"Let the fuck go," Derek yells. I then hear the knife hit the floor and scrape away. I instantly bend down on the floor to try and get the knife. I then feel a blow to my side, causing me to scream in pain. I see Derek has kicked me, he's leaning forward trying to find the knife.

"Don't you fucking touch her," Kyle growls and he lands on top of Derek, punching him in the jaw. I hear Derek moan. Kyle hits him again and again, Derek quickly bites Kyle's arm and kicks him in the stomach, making him fall over, grunting. I feel the stinging pain in my side, but I can't let Derek get that knife. I crawl forward and I see something shine from under a cabinet. I quickly look at Derek and see he is a few feet away from me, looking for it, I then see Kyle jump him again. They are both distracted, I reach for it under the cabinet and I feel the tip of the knife, I'm struggling to fully reach it. I push my hand harder, trying to guide it closer to me. I think I got it when I feel my hair being grabbed, I then feel my face bash against the floor. My eyes go blurry by the force. I feel Derek's hand next to mine reaching for the knife. I shake my head, I quickly knee him in his groin, and his hand goes straight there, cupping himself. I quickly grab the knife and start to crawl away. I wasn't fast enough as Derek is on top of me again. He's trying to grab the knife, but I stretch my arm above my head, trying to keep it out of reach.

"Give it up," Derek grunts. I try with all my might to keep him away, but with his weight, I'm struggling. I look to my side and see Kyle laying on the floor, his face is badly beaten, I see a wooden statue near his head. Oh God, Kyle. Is he ok?

"Fuck you," I spit in his eyes. He momentarily sits up to rub the spit away. I then feel a smack against my face. I scream again. I feel the pain shoot all over my face. I know I dropped the knife by the impact.

"What a shame. It wasn't meant to be like this. But now I can't get away with this anymore. So I better take you both down with me." I can hardly register his words. The punch he gave me has left me dazed. When my vision clears a little, I see Derek on top of me raising the knife. I open my eyes wide with horror. I'm going to be stabbed again. I can't escape death twice. I turn my head so my last vision will be of Kyle. I look and see that he's gone. I then hear Derek scream. I look back to see Kyle standing above Derek, he has knocked Derek out unconscious. He falls off me to the floor.

"I got you," Kyle says groggily and I can't help but throw myself at him. I let all the tears fall down. I cry for what we both went through. I look at Derek on the floor. I can't believe what has happened. I feel like I'm dreaming, like this is another nightmare, but I don't wake up. This is real. Caitlin stabbed me for Kyle, Derek was willing to do it for me. When did our lives get so fucked up?

twenty-six

Kyle and I are at the hospital getting checked out. I have a few bruises, but Kyle wasn't as lucky. He was knocked over the head, so he is getting a C. T. scan to make sure there's no damage. I'm sitting in the waiting room when my parents run in. When they see me, they sprint to me and hug me for dear life. I can feel my mom crying for me. I can't help but cry with her. We cried for what seemed like ages.

"How's Kyle?" Dad asks. I can't help the tear that falls.

"He's getting a scan to make sure there is no damage, he was bashed in the head, so they are just taking precautions.

"Honey, look at you," Mom cries. She trails her finger over my left cheek. When I went to the bathroom, I saw the huge black and blue mark on my cheek, my eye is a little bruised and swollen, too. Good thing Mom can't see my side, it's covered in the biggest black bruise imaginable. When I walk, I can feel the pain.

"What happened?" Dad asks.

"Yes, we would like to know what happened, too, please Miss." I turn to see the same two detectives who was investigating what was happening last time. Detective Anders and Detective Roninson.

"Hi, Alison, sorry you had to go through all of this, especially what you went through before. Can you please tell us what happened tonight?" Detective Anders asks.

"Well, I went to Derek's to hang out, I started texting Kyle. When Derek found out, he wasn't happy, when I told him me and Kyle got back together, he just flipped. He was going on about how we were meant to be together. He admitted about the letters, photos, and the dog." I hear my mom gasp beside me.

"Go on, what happened next?" Detective Roninson says.

"While he was saying all this stuff, he was pacing, so I called Kyle from my pocket, I was yelling at Derek so he could hear me, to come help me, but Derek knew what I was doing. Because he knew Kyle was coming, he was planning to do to him what Caitlin did to me." I take a deep breath. Just retelling it was hard to do, I can't help the tears that start to fall.

"Please go on." Detective Anders insists.

"We heard Kyle pull up, he looked through the window and saw me on the floor crying, he was banging on the door. Derek was behind waiting for Kyle to enter, when the door opened, I went by instinct. I charged at Derek, we all fought for the knife, it dropped, and we struggled to get it first. In the process, I got booted on my side and punched in the face, he connected my face to the ground. I didn't see him knock Kyle out, but I saw Kyle on the floor, not moving with a wooden statue next to him. I kneed Derek when he was reaching for the knife, but couldn't do more. Derek got the knife and he was about to stab me. I thought I was to die, I turned so I can see Kyle, I wanted him to be the last thing I saw, but he was gone. I then hear Derek yell out, then he is on the floor unconscious." I cry finishing off what happened. My mom and dad hold me.

"Thank you, Alison, again, sorry you had to go through all that," Anders says.

"What happens now?" Dad asks.

"Well, we will get a statement from Kyle to back it up, but Derek is going to be locked away for a long time. He is eighteen so he will be charged. Admitting about the letters, especially the dog, that will be on top of this as well. The charges of the dog and that will be taken off Caitlin. She admitted she never did those things, this is the proof she was telling the truth. We will keep you informed when Derek is locked up. He is somewhere in this hospital, but don't worry we have two policemen at his door. He's not going anywhere." Anders says.

"Thank God," Mom whispers.

"Thank you for your time, feel better," Roninson says and both detectives stand up. We say our goodbyes.

We wait for what feels like hours and when I see a doctor walk toward us, I stand up automatically. You always look for signs when it comes to doctors, you look at their eyes to get some clue as to what to expect. When I do, I see a small smile, his eyes are emotionless. Probably from all the bad news he's had to give, but I don't want bad news. I won't accept it.

"How is he?" I ask when he's a few feet away from me.

"He's doing good. The scans came back clear, no brain trauma. Just a very large bump. He's going to feel that for a while. He is covered in bruises but nothing serious. He has to try and stay awake for the next 12 hours, so you have to keep an eye on him. It's just a precaution." I sigh in relief, I feel so relieved. He's going to be ok, thank the holy Jesus.

"Can we go see him?"

"Sure, he's been asking for you anyway. Stubborn young man." I can't help but laugh.

"Yeah, he is."

When we get to Kyle's room, he is sitting on the bed, putting on his T-shirt. I can't help but see the bruises cover his body, but he is still gorgeous. When he sees me, he gets off the bed and runs to me, holding me like I'm going to disappear any second. I hold him just as tightly. I can't help the tear that escapes. I don't know what I would have done if something happened to him.

"Hey, why are you crying? I'm fine. Just waiting for the paperwork and we can go." Kyle says, stroking my hair.

"I thought I lost you when I saw you on the floor, not moving, I felt my whole world crumble away." I can't help the tears that follow.

"Shhh, I'm ok, we are ok."

"Thank you for protecting my little girl. I can never repay you for what you have done," Dad says from behind me, I step back, but Kyle has his arm around my waist. I flinch a little, but don't want him to let me go.

"I love her, would die for her," Kyle says the last part looking into my eyes, and I know he is serious. They shake hands, and my mom hugs Kyle, he winces in pain by how tight the hug was, she had to apologize over and over.

"What the fuck? Hell the fuck, fuckity fuck happened?" I hear Lex yell when she enters the room. Her eyes go wide when she sees the state of me and Kyle. "What the fuck?" Lex says looking between us both,

"How did you know we were here?" Yeah, first question I had to ask.

"Your Mom called, glad she did. Now, what the hell happened?"

"Derek." Just saying the name causes my body to shudder.

"Derek?" Lex looks disbelieved. We tell her what happened. By the end of it, she is in tears, and we are holding each other.

"You need to stop facing death, going to have a heart attack by the time I'm twenty. I never liked Derek, told you there was something about him I didn't like. I must have sensed his psychotic side. So happy he is going to be locked up."

"I don't plan on people trying to hurt me you know. Unfortunately, I'm a magnet for them."

"No more drawing in psychotic killers," Lex says poking me with her finger.

"I'll try. If you sense anything bad towards anyone, I will listen. Got college next year, that's a whole lot of strangers."

"That's it, you're not going to college. Just decided. You are staying in your room, never leaving." We all turn to stare at my dad, we all burst out laughing. "I'm serious," he says.

"I know you are Gerald, but you know that's not going to happen."
Mom says patting his shoulder, she looks at me giving me a smile, but
I can see the sadness in her eyes. She doesn't want me to leave either.

"I'm not leaving yet. Let's just get this paperwork filled out ASAP
and get out of here, I'm sick of hospitals."

"Here, here. I'll go find a nurse and give her a kick in the ass to
hurry up." Lex says as she leaves the room.

"I love you." I look up at Kyle and smile at his words.

"I love you, too." He smiles down at me and kisses my lips softly,
not caring my parents are still in the room.

"No more kissing my daughter. Ready to leave this place as well,"
Dad says. After five minutes, a nurse comes in, and Kyle fills out his
release forms. We all head to my house. None of us want to be separat-
ed. Kyle has to stay up just to make sure he doesn't have a concussion.
I can tell he is tired, but we all try and keep each other entertained.
What a weekend. I lose my virginity yesterday, almost get killed today. Hopefully tomorrow is a normal stress-free day, as Sunday is the
day of rest.

We get a call from Detective Anders the following day before dinner saying that Derek has admitted to all charges, he is going to be
locked up without bail. He is charged with attempted murder to both
Kyle and I. I sit at the table, telling the news to everyone, I still feel
like it didn't happen. It's Derek. I see images of him in my head. Being
there for me, defending me. He was talking about a dark road, that's
hard to come back from. Was he on that road? I still don't get how he
thought that I would agree to fit into his perfect future plan. I'm glad I
was never pressured for a certain future,

It's Caitlin's hearing tomorrow, my parents have tried to persuade
me to not go, especially after everything that has happened with Derek,
but I feel I still need to. I want my closure with Caitlin. I need to move
on with my life. Kyle supported my decision, and told me he will drive
me there, and wait in the parking lot for me. He doesn't want to see
her. I can't imagine what he thinks when it comes to Caitlin, but I now
have a little idea as I experienced it with Derek. Tomorrow, tomorrow

is the end of the horrible chapter in my life.

twenty-seven

I'm sitting outside the courtroom, and I feel like I'm going to have a panic attack any second. It's already started, but I haven't worked up the courage to go inside yet. Kyle is sitting next to me holding my hand. When we were told the hearing was about to begin, I told Kyle I wasn't ready, he didn't need any more explanation, we sat down, and that was about ten minutes ago. I'm looking at the door, and I know I will come back out better or worse. I need to do this, I keep telling myself that. I just keep seeing images of Caitlin from my nightmares, to her hooking up with Kyle, her standing in front of me, staring at me, but I knew it always ended the same, her stabbing me. The last few nightmares though were different, I think subconsciously that I knew it was Derek behind me. It was him towards the end, but still seeing her looking at me, that's what I keep seeing in my head. What if I go in and all my nightmares will become reality?

I need to be strong, but why do I feel so weak? I have to put up with so much the last few months, I have come out the other side, still breathing, coping. I don't want to cope anymore, I want to forget all of this, put it behind me. Kyle squeezes my hand, I turn to look up and see all the love shine from his eyes. He isn't judging me, he knows I will do this when I'm ready. I stand up and take a deep breath.

"You can do this," Kyle says and I nod, I walk to the door that takes me to the room the hearing is taking place. When I put my hand on the handle, I turn and see Kyle is waiting for me to enter. I asked him if he wanted to come in with me when he was driving us here, but he said no. I didn't want to push him, but I knew he was taking the whole Caitlin thing hard, he was close to her, I get it. I take one final deep breath and walk in.

I see a few empty spaces, and I decide to sit in the middle. I don't want her to notice me if I can help it, but when I look up I see her at the stand and she is staring at me. I feel my throat tighten up. Of course she is going to notice me walk in, I interrupted the hearing to sit down. When I look into her eyes, it isn't the same as what I saw in my dreams. In my dreams, her eyes were either dark, angry or emotionless. Now I see the pain and guilt. She has tears in her eyes. I know by just looking at her how sorry she is. I knew I made the right choice of coming.

When Caitlin was asked to explain what happened that night of the dance, I leaned forward, as I want to know what was going through her head. I need to know her reason. I knew it was over Kyle, but there's a line you don't cross when it comes to close to killing someone, no matter how in love you are with someone.

"At the dance everything was fine, I was enjoying myself. I enjoyed getting ready, being part of the girls. My friends, no offense to them, suck up to me because they think I'm going places when I'm older due to how smart I am. Even though, I messed that up now. Even my smarts didn't help me prevent doing the most stupid thing of my life," Caitlin looks down and takes a few deep breaths. "I believed I was in love with Kyle Jacobs. Can't tell you how long as I'm not sure when it happened, but I have been in love with him for a couple of years. We were close. He talked to me, he told me things he couldn't tell his other best friend. The girl he grew up with. I knew he was close to her, too. In my head I assumed he saw her as a sister, as he hooked up with many other girls. He told me he wasn't ready to settle down, he wanted to enjoy his high school years. I got that, I understood it, think I accepted it as I knew the girls meant nothing to him."

"I knew things were changing between Kyle and Alison. I saw how he wanted to be around her more, how he was looking at her. I thought he wouldn't pursue it. He put her on a high pedestal. I was relieved when she started dating Derek Wilson, I thought maybe I still stood a chance. He even told me that himself, Alison and Lex would be going to the same college, would be nice if I came. I took it as a childish twelve-year-old way that maybe there was hope for us. I took the little things and made it sound in my head that it meant more. When they finally got together, yes I was jealous, I was hurt. I knew I couldn't compete with her. He wouldn't look at me the way he looked at her. I started to accept it. I even lied and said I started dating someone else. I was pathetic, but I didn't want them to think there was something wrong, I was hurting. I tried to hide it well," Caitlin says tears flowing down her cheeks, I can't help but cry with her.

"At the dance, we were all laughing. Kyle and I were dancing, talking and I hated that I wasn't going to end up with him. The thing that hurt more was when Alison and I were in the bathroom. I looked at her and all I thought was how this shy girl who wore clothes far too big, turned into this gorgeous, beautiful young woman. I saw all the good in her, I was even jealous of that. She was being so nice to me, I was hurting that she got the person I was in love with. I knew she loved him, too, but I wouldn't accept it. When she said she was leaving, I knew they were leaving to make love. I left the bathroom a few minutes after Alison. I watched her walk towards Kyle, I saw his eyes shine when he saw her. I felt all this anger, this hurt, all this jealousy build up. I just saw them making love in my head, I couldn't let it happen," Caitlin is proper crying, it's getting harder for her to finish what happened. I see all this in my head, I knew she liked Kyle, but never once thought she was hurting.

"I felt like I wasn't me anymore, I felt like I was watching myself pick up the knife. I was yelling at myself, 'what am I doing?'

But I couldn't hear the words. I started walking really fast, I then just charged at her. I felt the knife slide in, I couldn't believe I did it, couldn't believe it when I did it again. I knew it wasn't me. I know I'm not that person, but feel my brain switched off. My mind is all hazy after that, I didn't feel the two policemen grab me, I didn't see Alison on the floor. When I came back to my senses, I was in a cell. I felt like I dreamt it all but knew I didn't when I saw the blood all over my costume. I was wearing black, but yet I could see it, smell it. I knew part of me was broken.

"Alison was good to me, and I hurt her. She never did anything wrong. She loved the same guy as me, I guess it all built up inside of me. I am so sorry, I know it would never take what happened away. I have to live with the nightmares, I see what happened over and over in my head. I have to live with this forever. I am sorry, I'm so sorry Alison, I didn't mean to hurt you," Caitlin looks at me, pleading with me, I am crying with her. I feel her pain, she has been suffering with me. She's had her own demons. She and Derek are different, she felt remorse, as Derek didn't.

"I forgive you," I yell out, and I see Caitlin cry even more. Do I forgive her? I don't know. How can you forgive someone who almost killed you? But I know it would help her, give her some closure. I know I got mine. I know I will probably still have the odd nightmare, but I know it won't affect me as it once did. I know I'm stronger for doing this. I stay till I see what they sentence her with. She got five years in a psychiatric ward, they accept she wasn't in her right frame of mind. Her going from a steady background, loving parents, good home life, straight A student, to a breakdown episode. At least I know she feels guilty for what she did. Most people would want jail time for what she did, but I got what I wanted, Closure.

I told my parents, Lex, and Kyle what happened, I retold them what Caitlin said. No one said anything more about it. I told them I got my closure, I think they are happy that some good came out of me going. I know Lex isn't happy, she wanted Caitlin locked up, and the key thrown away, but I know I am able to move forward now. I want to finish off my school year and enjoy the rest of my high school experience. I know when school starts up again, I will once again be number one topic of gossip. I think I'm starting to accept it. Hopefully, no more drama happens and everyone forgets about me. I want to be invisible again, I have Kyle and Lex, that's all I need. I wanted to have more friends, be noticed. I got my wish but didn't turn out as I expected. The only good thing that happened is me and Kyle.

I asked Kyle once if I didn't have my makeover and started getting attention from other guys if he would have made a move on me. He told me that we were always meant to be together. That maybe he might have taken him time to build up the courage to admit his feelings for me, he knew he would have. He knew I was it for him, as I knew he was it for me. I started wearing Kyle's old T-shirts, I only wear them when I'm stopping at Kyle's, as I know Lex would have a fit if I went back to my old fashion ensembles. I feel when I wear them, I am closer to the old me. I know I will never be that girl. I have gone through so much in just a short few months, but I am stronger. I am free from my anger.

We all put Derek and Caitlin behind us and decide to focus on Christmas. As this will be our last Christmas in our house, Mom goes all out. Each room has decorations. Mom bought the biggest turkey you can imagine. Is she cooking for twenty? I know it is hard for all of us that this will no longer be our home. Kyle has taken it harder as he hates I won't be next door to him. That I will be living across town. The house isn't even sold yet, and he's acting like I've moved already. When I start to put presents under the tree, I see the present I got for Derek. I look at it and hate how he turned out. I hate what he put me through. Picking up the gift, I grab my coat and head out the door. I walk to the river, near the running path I normally took, and throw it. I watch it sink, just like our friendship.

twenty-eight

Kyle stayed with me on Christmas Eve, Dad didn't like it. Mom explained about me staying over every Friday at Kyle's, but it's apparently different when it's under his roof. I woke up on Christmas morning feeling Kyle's lips kissing my neck, and I can't help but smile. What a wonderful way to wake up in the morning.

"Merry Christmas beautiful," Kyle says against my neck, he continues to kiss my neck, and jaw. I can't help but sigh.

"Merry Christmas. What a wonderful way to wake up. It should be like this every morning," I stretch.

"Don't think your Dad would approve." I can't help but laugh. Dad never had a say about Kyle spending the night. Mom and I out voted him, he had to deal with it. I wouldn't have sex with them in the house. I read too many books and watched too many movies on parents catching their children at it, there is no way I'm letting that happen to me. The way Kyle is teasing me, I'm about to throw all logic out the window.

"Wake up you two, I know you're awake," Mom knocks on the door and yells out. I can't help but groan.

"She psychic or something?" I can't help but laugh again, I use to think that when it came to my mother.

"No, we are just predictable." I kiss Kyle on the lips and get out of bed. I grab the things I need and head for the shower.

I try and not take to long as I know my parents will be waiting for us. Kyle needs a shower, too. When I walk back into my room, Kyle isn't there. I assume he must have went downstairs. I dressed in the bathroom, think Dad would mind if I dressed with Kyle watching me, even though I know Kyle would enjoy the view. Talking about views, Kyle walks in wearing a pair of faded blue jeans that sits on his hips and he's shirtless. I see some drops of water sliding down his chest, all I want to do is lick him. I lick my lips at the thought.

"Babe, you need to stop looking at me like that, or I am going to have to take you against your door. I don't care if your parents hear us," Kyle growls. I shake my head trying to clear my lustful thoughts. God how much I want him to do that. I definitely want to try it against the wall. We always make out against them, can just imagine him being inside me, thrusting harder and harder.

"Babe, stop it." Kyle has pinned me against the wall. My hands automatically go to his chest. God he is so hard and firm. "I want you so badly. I need to be inside you." Kyle says against my ear. I let out a moan.

"Stop whatever you two are doing, and get your butts down here," Mom yells up the stairs. Kyle leans his forehead against me and groans, and I can't help the giggle that leaves me.

"Mama 2 is a cock blocker." I can't help but laugh. Kyle laughs with me. He puts on a light blue T-shirt, and I quickly tie my hair up in a high ponytail, it's still wet from the shower. We head downstairs, hand in hand.

"By the way, where did you shower?" Did he use my parents?

"Why, you wanted to join me?" Kyle waggles his eyebrows. I hit him in the chest.

"No, I just thought you were going to use the one I used."

"I used your old bathroom," I stop at the bottom of the stairs and look at him.

"Why would you go in that room? That room gives me the creeps." I can't help but shiver.

"I needed a shower, didn't want to take longer waiting for you to finish. I just went in there. Didn't think much of it. It still looks how it used to." Kyle pulls me into him, hugging me. "I hate that he ruined your room, your house."

"I know, me too. I just can't go in that room, I just see the image of how it looked last time. I just can't live in it anymore. Bet you think I'm pathetic."

"What, never. I get it. Didn't think I would upset you. I'm sorry."

"'Don't be silly, it's my issue, not yours. Let's go have Christmas breakfast before my dad has a heart attack, as I bet he is imagining you having your wicked way with me."

"I wish," Kyle says, and we laugh to the kitchen.

After breakfast, we pile into the living room and start to hand out presents. Five minutes into it, Lex bangs the door open and lets herself in as she owns the place.

"You guys couldn't wait for me? Feel the love," Lex says as she plunks herself down on the couch.

"Didn't think you would be here so early," I say. I can't help but roll my eyes at her. She helps herself to the glass of orange juice that is on the coffee table.

"Well, parents were doing my head in. Mom was crying that this will be my last Christmas before I go to college. Only so many tears and reminiscing of me as a baby I could handle." We knew Lex was coming here so her presents from us to her are under the tree, too. Lex dropped off her presents a couple of days ago. When there're no more presents to hand out, we all start to unwrap our gifts. Why do I always feel like I'm twelve when opening presents? I get so excited.

"You're too cute," I hear Kyle say smiling at me.

"What? Why?"

"How your eyes have brightened up as you open up your gifts. It's so cute." Kyle leans forward and gives me a soft kiss.

"You two get a room," Lex groans.

"No, don't get a room. Stop making out with my daughter. Trying to enjoy my presents here." I laugh at Dad.

We all open our gifts and tell each other what we have received. My mom got earrings and matching neckless from Dad. Perfume from Kyle, and lingerie from Lex, who winked at her, causing my dad to blush. I couldn't help but giggle. Leave it to Lex to get my mom something like that.

"Keep your love life fresh," Lex shrugs that it's no big deal.

Dad got a new golf set from Mom, which made Dad jump up and down like a school girl. Kyle got him some vintage Scotch. Dad never asked how he got it as he's under age. Think he got help from his parents. Lex got him a box that said Kink up your life. It involved a silk blindfold, silk scarves for tying up, a whip, and some lubrication. I look at the gift with my mouth open. Why would she get him that? I have never seen my dad look so red with embarrassment in my life.

"What? Thought it was a great gift," we all look a Lex.

"Gerald, we will try it when they go off to college," Mom whispers, but we all hear her. Kyle and I groan as Lex cheers Mom on. Think Dad is shocked by what Mom said as his mouth is hanging open, she just winks at him.

Lex got some hoop earrings, a white silk blouse, a new iPad, leather boots she has been eying up. Which she squealed in delight. Kyle received expensive aftershave, iPod system. I got mac pro laptop, which I love as I know it will be useful for college. I tell my parents how much I love it. Lex got me leather pants and leather boob tube, my dad almost blew a gasket when he saw it. I assured him I won't wear it till I'm at college, but that makes him hate it more. I know I can't wait to try it on, it looks so badass. Kyle gave me a silver locket. I open it up and see one side is a picture of my parents, the other is a picture of Lex, Kyle and I. I love it. There's an inscription on the back.

My always

I swear I have tears in my eyes when I see it. It's perfect. I kiss Kyle hard on the lips, I pull apart when I hear my dad in what sounds like a coughing fit. My parents are standing up when I stop them.

"There's still one gift I have to give you guys," I say and I quickly run to my room and come back down. I'm holding an envelope and a box. I hand over the envelope to my parents. "It's for both of you." I watch my mom open it up as Dad watches. I hear Mom gasp.

"Two tickets to Paris," Mom whispers. Dad takes the card and reads it. It's two tickets and hotel reservation to Paris for New Year's.

"Princess, we can't accept this," Dad says.

"You guys can. You are the best parents I could ever ask for. You had to put up with so much, this is me thanking you. Please accept it. If you don't, it will hurt my feelings." I quiver my lips for effect.

"Such blackmail." Dad chuckles at me.

"I know." I can't help but laugh. Mom squeezes me saying it's the best gift ever.

"Even better than mine? I feel offended." Lex says. I can't help the snort that leaves me.

"Lex your gifts were very imaginative, that's for sure." Mom tells her and goes into the kitchen. I take Kyle's hand and tell him I want to give him his gift outside. He follows me. Hear Lex groan again but I ignore her. She's just as sickly when James is around.

When we get to the swing, I hand over the box and sit down. I watch him open the box slowly. I hold my breath as I watch him take out the chain, looking at the pendant.

"St. Christopher?" I nod.

"When I saw it, I was drawn to it. The woman at the store says it's meant to hold protection to the wearer." I tell him the story behind it. "You helped me carry my pain, you saved me." I don't know why, but I feel tears building up. God, why am I crying?

"I love it," I see Kyle put it on. I hold the necklace he gave me that is against my chest. My always. Kyle kisses my lips softly. "I love you."

"I love you, too, always have."

Epilogue

"Look at this place, it's our freedom," I hear Lex squeal behind me, holding a box. I laugh at her.

"Yeah, we lucked out when we found this place." I walk through the front door with a box of my things in my hands.

"Think of all the new drama, the new hot guys to window shop. We need to make sure we stomp down any bitches that get in our way. Think you should throw one of your famous punches and word will get around not to mess with us," I can't help but laugh.

"Hopefully there is no drama, I'm not going to throw any punches." Well, unless they try to get it on with Kyle.

"Such a party pooper."

"How many more boxes are there? Told you we should have left sooner," Dad complains, walking back and forth carrying boxes and furniture.

"I slept in, so sue me," Lex says. I walk to what will be my new room. I set the box down and go to the window. I see the gorgeous view of a fountain. I can imagine sitting here reading a new book. I then feel arms wrap around my waist.

"Think your Dad is going to kill Lex any second." I chuckle at the thought.

"Long as they do it quietly, trying to enjoy my new home."

"Our new home," Kyle says against my ear, causing my whole body to shiver.

"Our home." It's two weeks till we start classes at UCLA. Yes, we all got accepted. This was all of our first choices, and we got in. It took us four weeks till we found a place that will be our new home for four years. We found a three bedroom house that's twenty minutes away from the college. The place itself is spacious and perfect in every aspect. When we told Dad that we decided we all wanted to live together, Dad wasn't happy. He didn't like that Kyle and I were going to be sharing a bed every day, but he got over it. Kyle and I share a room, Lex and James share one.

Yes, they are still holding strong. He applied for UCLA and Lex was happy he got accepted. Don't know what she would have done if he didn't. Just glad that none of us had to go through that. The third bedroom is a spare room/study. We thought if anyone visited or stayed over we had the space. Lex says that if the guys fall out of line that's where they will be sleeping.

"Can't believe we are finally here, college. We did it." Remember when we went back to school after Christmas holidays, we were the number one topic. Everyone talked about Derek going psychotic. None of Derek's friends would go near me, apart from Tom, but knew he felt awkward around me. Don't think any of them knew what was going through his head. They couldn't accept that their friend would do something like that.

After a few months, all gossip died down, well about us anyway. I worked my little butt off, but I made time for parties, as I still wanted to have the high school experience. I even accidentally got drunk with Lex when we were drinking some punch that got spiked. We had to stay at Kyle's, and poor Kyle had to nurse us both. Things finally went back to normal. My childhood home got sold, my parents have moved into a recently built home. It has an amazing garden, which my mom spends a lot of time tending.

"We are here, next chapter of our lives," Kyle says, he spins me around and kisses my lips. I never thought I would have ended up with Kyle Jacobs, my best friend, my next door neighbor. We went through so much, but we got here in the end. Where we were supposed to be.

When we walk on campus to get our class schedules, I look at all the buildings and pray I don't get lost. I see other freshman walking around looking star struck like me, least I have my two best friends to help me. Lex and I quickly go to a coffee stand to get out latte fix. When we walk back to where the guys are, a group of girls are flirting with our men. We've only been gone a few minutes and they are already surrounded by no shame girls.

"I don't fucking think so," Lex growls as we march to them. My sentiments exactly. "Move hussies, these guys are ours." Lex slides in and James wraps his arm around her waist. Kyle walks towards me taking my hand and pulling me against him.

"Sorry girls, like we said, we are taken," Kyle says smiling down at me.

I feel the tingles by his words, but I see the girls sizing Lex and I up, thinking if we are much competition. One girl is looking at Kyle like she could jump him at any second. She sees me glaring at her and she smirks at me, the bitch smirks at me. I know what she is thinking. Savannah had the same look back in her bully days. It's the look that she thinks that she can tempt Kyle away. Savannah and I have stayed in touched surprisingly, we got closer the last half of the school year. Lex tolerates her, but I'm more forgiving.

"Well, if you ever change your mind. See you around." The bitch seductively says before walking away. I know I already hate her with a passion. I know I have to watch out for her.

"Hate that bitch," Lex says. I nod in agreement. "Do we need to babysit you boys? Gone for coffee and you're attacked by girls." James nuzzles her neck.

"Don't worry babe, you know you're it for me," James says.

"You have nothing to worry about Als. You're my always." Kyle presses his finger against my forehead, relaxing it. "I can see the angry lines," Kyle says in explanation. We start walking and get in line where the schedules are to be picked up. The guy in front of me turns around when he sees me and gives me a charming smile. I feel Kyle pull me against his chest. I hear Lex chuckle behind me.

"Looks like I'm not the only person who is being checked out." I can't help but smile that Kyle is just as possessive.

Well, great start for the college year. Wonder what the years here are going to bring. Long as I have Kyle and Lex at my side, I know I can handle anything thrown my way. Hopefully.

Acknowledgments

Thank You! Thank You! Thank You!

I want to thank you, the readers first. I hope you enjoyed the continued journey of Alison and Kyle. Thank you for giving my book a chance. You have helped support me, believed in me, you have no idea how much I appreciate it. All the messages and posts you send me, telling me how much you loved A Simple Change, and that you all were dying for book 2. It filled my heart with such warmth knowing you enjoyed something that I worked so hard to accomplish and love. The readers on my author page you all rock, you are my stars.

Again I want to thank Daniel for being there for me, encouraging me to follow my dream and write what is in my head. Putting up with me talking none stop about my book and my ideas. Thank you for putting up that most of our conversation was about The Hardest of Changes. To my lovely gorgeous little boy Jake, thank you for putting up with a busy mommy. I love you dearly.

To my beta readers, you have put up with me and let me bite your ear off. Thank you for helping me make this book best it can be. All the notes and advice were so much appreciated, I have learned so much through each of you. I'm so happy that we have become friends. You have no choice now but to beta read every book I write, just warning you. Thank you, Hannah, Mindy, Beth, Patti and Karen. You're all my bright sexy stars.

Thank you to Lauren, Bernie, Richard, Fran, Paula, Laura, Naomi 1, Naomi 2, Valerie, Jennie, Judy, Hayley, Stephie and Autumn thank you for supporting me.

To the amazing people who have answered all my non-stop questions, Laura at Editing For You, Pink Ink Designs, and N.K Author

Services. Thank you for making my book look amazing. I don't know what I would have done without you.

Jen Wildner, thank you for helping me share the love of my books, you are a Godsend.

Again thank you for reading my book, thank you for giving me a chance <3 <3

The next book I will be working on is a stepbrother romance. Look out for its release.

A Simple Change Buy Links

Amazon US: http://tiny.cc/aSimpleChange-AmazonUS
Amazon UK: http://tiny.cc/aSimpleChange-AmazonUK
B&N: http://www.barnesandnoble.com/w/books/1121380940...

About The Author

J.L. Ostle was born in Antrim, Northern Ireland and was raised as an Army brat. She is now living in Carlisle England. J.L Ostle is a full-time mother looking after her cute, active three-year-old boy.

When she hasn't got her head stuck in a book or writing, she's watching movies, hanging with friends. J.L has a little obsession with Supernatural. She enjoys catching up on her TV shows Vampire Diaries, Big Bang Theory, Geordie Shore and Grimm.

Connect with me

I enjoy messages and posts you send me, so have any questions, or want to talk about any of the books, drop me a line x x

Facebook
www.facebook.com/J.L.OSTLE
Goodreads
www.goodreads.com/author/show/12682033.J_L_Ostle
mazon
www.amazon.com/author/j.l.ostle

Made in the USA
Charleston, SC
08 September 2015